Wandering with Nathaniel

A Prayer for the Awakening of Humanity

David K. Munson

Nous Voice Communications, LLC
Chesterland, Ohio

Published in the United States by Nous Voice Communications

Copyright © 2023 by Nous Voice Communications, LLC

Cover Photo at Sunnybrook Preserve—Geauga Park District

All rights reserved. No part of this book may be reproduced in any manner, or for any reason without the express permission of the publisher. Exceptions to this guideline include: (1) Section 107 of the US Copyright Law allows for and defines fair use of original content. As such, we have used referenced and cited quotes in this book, and in the same light, we allow the fair use of original content from this material, as long as the length does not exceed fifty words, and the author/title is properly acknowledged; and (2) The use or reproduction of the poetry and metaphors in this work requires explicit permission from the publisher, except *When Souls Kiss*, which may be used in its entirety without permission at wedding ceremonies with proper author/title credits cited. Failure to comply with the above terms and guidelines may expose you to legal action. If you would like permission to use material from the book, please contact the publisher at *ourteam@nousvoice.com*. Thank you for your support of the author's original content and right of intellectual property.

ISBNs	Softcover	(1st edition)	979-8-9888821-0-7
	eBook	(1st edition)	979-8-9888821-1-4
	Audiobook	(1st edition)	979-8-9888821-2-1

Printed in the United States by Activities Press, Mentor, Ohio

First Edition: August 2023

This is a work of nonfiction. All the stories in this book are based upon the author's actual experiences. Some names and certain facts have been modified to protect the anonymity of those who may have a different perspective of the experiences described within.

Contents

Preface

Chapter One:	Soul Searching	1
Chapter Two:	My Fourth Grade Teacher	25
Chapter Three:	A Yellow Rocking Chair	39
Chapter Four:	Baseball and Guardian Angels	61
Chapter Five:	An Angel, an Ant, and Me	81
Chapter Six:	Our Creek	119
Chapter Seven:	Riding Shotgun	145
Chapter Eight:	Lost and Found	165
Chapter Nine:	The Train to Susquehanna	191
Chapter Ten:	A Glimpse of the Hereafter	223
Chapter Eleven:	Lost and Found Redux	243
Chapter Twelve:	The Orb of White Light	269
Epilogue:	A Prayer for Humanity	283

Acknowledgements

I have been blessed with a personal relationship with my guardian angel, Nathaniel, all my life. We have been together since the herebefore and will be together in the hereafter—when my present physical journey on Earth is done.

I was blessed to be surrounded by an army of angels as I wrote this book. They even inspired all the poems in this book, except *I'll Play Baseball in Heaven*. I wrote that one all by myself!

And to my female guardian angel who saved me from certain death many times. Truly, I would not be here without her.

Thank you to my sisters, Karen and Sue—we have always been there for each other. And to Nan and Pop, who always made me feel safe.

And to my cousins and best friends—we had so many adventures growing up that Huck Finn would have been jealous.

To my beta readers, Erica, Erin, Gail, Karen, Louise, and Sherry, who lovingly supplied the grit that polishes a final manuscript.

And finally, to my wife Dianne. I would not have completed this book without her love, inspiration, guidance, and professional editing experience. And considering all the different lifetimes we have already shared; this lifetime has been the most fulfilling.

Preface

Every year, we honor the completion of another trip around our Sun. In our minds, we perceive that we have orbited in a circle to the exact spot we were a year earlier. Behind the scenes, so to speak, is our galaxy propelling through the vast space of the universe at 8,575 miles per second. That's 4.5 billion miles every year! By the time you read through this whole book, many of you will have traveled more than 100 million miles through the Milky Way on spaceship Earth. Every second brings our planet, and us, into a different position within the Milky Way. Every second brings us to a place where new perspectives are possible. Every second brings us to a place where our journey continues into the unknown.

This book is based on real events of my life, and I hope that my experiences bring you toward whatever is next in your own life's journey. The interpretations of my experiences are solely mine. Please feel free to ignore, contemplate, or integrate at whatever level creates peacefulness in your life. You have your own perspectives from which you view the world. You have your own perceptions of your past and of our present shared reality.

I have added or modified non-critical details and changed some names along the way. For example, in chapter four, "As Kevin and Jack were leaving George's Market, I was already done with my Butterfinger ready to ride off, half expecting the manager to be running out to catch Kevin." I really don't remember which candy bar I purchased on that day, because I loved so many different ones. Were Kevin and Jack there? Yes, but I did change both their names. Were we at George's Supermarket on New Hackensack Road? Absolutely. Was that the day an angel came and saved our lives? Most definitely.

Those are the details I recall with extreme accuracy. Those are the moments in life ingrained in each of us—near-death experiences, spiritual encounters, serendipity, or *odd* coincidences that change the course of our lives. Those are the events we go over and over in our minds for days, weeks, months, years—just trying to find meaning in the details of those life-changing events. I really don't know what I did the day before those events. The unbelievable in this book is what's real! Ingrained in my memory. Burned into my soul. My guardian angel, Nathaniel, and I pray, in your own life's journey, you find your purpose, your healing, your awareness—aligned with your highest good—*with much less wandering than was in mine.*

The following metaphor focuses on our inability to see the world as it really is, and how disbelief can create our perceived reality:

> *There was a boy, Thomas, who grew up in a household that only had an AM radio that only tuned to one station. As he grew up into adulthood, he believed—and maybe would have staked his life on—the existence of only one radio station, 1100 AM Talk of the Country radio. It would have been blasphemy for anyone to challenge his long-held belief system by disclosing that there*

were really hundreds of other AM radio stations. And to reveal FM radio station frequencies existed—and they even played music—would have been met with extreme doubt.

One day, Thomas decided to leave his quiet existence and walk to town. On the way, he heard something different coming from a house he had never seen before. He rushed to the door and knocked to see if he could help. A woman answered the door and reassured Thomas that everything was just hunky-dory. She invited Thomas into her home to hear the music playing from her newfangled contraption—a Bose Wave Music System IV Stereo connected to her Sirius XM Satellite Radio account.

This cannot be, Thomas declared. There is only one true radio station—1100 AM Talk of the Country! And out of the house in disbelief he ran. The neighborly woman went out onto her porch just in time to see Thomas disappear into the isolated forest from which he came. As she returned into her home, she pulled out her iPhone and remotely turned down the volume on her new Bose Wave system. She said a prayer for Thomas' awakening and was hopeful that someday he would return.

Unlike Thomas in the above metaphor, awareness has never been a problem for me. I have lived my life hyper-aware—and it has been both a blessing and a curse, of sorts. When angels have touched your soul—calmed you from childhood fear, saved you from drowning, and altered your life path—it becomes easier to discern not-love from only-love. The two are not mutually exclusive. My heightened awareness of the light of only-love has brought me to places where not-love is easily discernable.

I have come to understand that you can simultaneously experience the blessings of Spirit and luckily remain a distant observer of not-love. You can still point out the darkness and remain energetically disconnected from it. It's the awareness of darkness that shows us how and where to focus our light!

I have met plenty of nice people who are oblivious to *both* the darkness *and* the light. I know many people who do not want to acknowledge the not-love in our world. Even some of the beta readers of my near-final manuscript encouraged me to write a book with *only* spiritual insights—only the Universal truths.

But as I have already stated, my hyper-awareness of the world has brought me to this place. A place where only-love can only be explained as a contrast to not-love—which I generally call in this book—the *darkness*. And yes, sometimes the messages from Spirit were overwhelming —full of confirmation that our present reality is a mess—but the messages were always full of love.

This required a lot of introspection on my part and made writing and editing this book very difficult at times. There were things I just couldn't get myself to write about. Things I wrote about and deleted. But most importantly, I prayed about it. I prayed about this journey.

Ultimately, the Universe encouraged me to include the information that might help awaken even one soul—no matter how controversial it may seem at the present time. And now, it is part of your spiritual journey. And that's exactly what I am doing here—awakening souls to the spiritual war presently in our time-space dimension. And the vastness of love—there's a lot of that in these writings.

We must pray that love will unite us—with all our perceived differences—into one human family. If by reading this book you experience just a glimpse of the darkness, your awakening will help you understand that the Universe needs your light to shine bright. We must pray for clarity. We must pray for awareness. We must pray to discern how best to shine our God-given soul light. Luckily, your heart and soul arrived here in this time-space dimension well equipped to discern what may have been fooling your mind.

When, not if, you get to the section that stops you in your tracks, or makes you feel uncomfortable, or confused, or in disbelief—that's the time I hope you will continue reading. Don't relegate the messages in this book to the dusty pile of unfinished life business. You never know when there might be an insight, a different way to look at life, or a healing lesson in there for *your* highest good. Spirit led me here. Spirit led you here, too. I wrote this book for *you*!

"We are all the leaves of one tree.
We are all the waves of one sea."

~Thich Nhat Hanh, Vietnamese Buddhist Monk

Wandering with Nathaniel

Chapter One
Soul Searching
A Spiritual Perspective on Soul-based Identity

Am I Worthy?

David K. Munson ©2021

*Am I worthy to stand on one foot
with left hand on head,
Gazing at the northern star,
for that is what was said.*

*For the reason next explained
I shall do this every night,
I am told I am a sinner
who needs to get it right.*

*My mind knows this ritual
will make my spirit whole,
More worthy of God's love.
Is it an unattainable goal?*

I never intended to write a book. My life plan was to have a career focused on cleaning up our damaged environment of toxic chemicals. One day, after doing just that for many years, I was in the front yard of my home doing some gardening under the flowering plum tree I had planted a year earlier. Out of nowhere, my guardian angel, Nathaniel, stated in no uncertain terms, "David, it's time to write your book." Not wanting to seem contradictory, I asked, "What book?" He replied matter-of-factly, "The reason you came here—to this life—at this time." Hmmm. I continued my gardening, which I loved because it was meditative, reduced my stress, and took my mind off losing my multimillion-dollar environmental cleanup company. Throughout the summer of 2001, Nathaniel would remind me often, as I gardened, it was time.

Honestly, Nathaniel was the only one, in my whole life, who truly understood me. I came into this world as a protector—of my family, of my friends, of the environment. But even a protector needs a protector, and Nathaniel stuck with me as we wandered through life—the good, the bad, the ugly, and what you will read about in this book—the unbelievable.

And that's why Nathaniel wanted me to begin to write—to set aside the secrecy we have lived with for more than fifty years. To shine the light of truth on my life experiences and their relationship to our shared existence. I never revealed these life experiences with anyone until well into my forties. The more I shared, the more others could relate because they had similar near-death experiences, visits from deceased loved ones, or angels saving their life. At a minimum, these people felt relief, and maybe some felt a healing they had yearned for, or maybe it just created a shared moment. But I am getting ahead of myself. So, allow me to start at the beginning.

I felt like a stranger in my own skin—a mystery to myself. I would stare at my hands, squeeze my fingers, and wonder how I got into this body. I could not help wondering why I was born with adult-sized ears on a child-sized head. Despite these feelings, I was certain I was more than skin, blood, cells, muscles, hair, fingers, ears, and toes. Well, as certain as an eight-year-old kid could be.

I wondered what special qualities made humans different from animals. Animals were also made up of skin, blood, cells, muscles, and hair. Why did I feel so disconnected? I theorized it must be that "soul thing" I had heard about in church, and I *was* separate from my body. That would explain why our bodies are buried in a cemetery and souls go to Heaven, *if we were good*. I figured I was good, since I always ate my vegetables, tried hard in school, played baseball, and was nice to other kids. I thought I would eventually be one of those people who went to Heaven.

So, I continued my search for the answer to my most pressing questions. Although I spent my time doing the things a normal eight-year-old kid does, I was always aware that the answers might come at any moment, during any activity. Sometimes, my body felt like a stiff suit, something you would wear, but not by choice. At other times, my body would seem to be on automatic pilot, and I would wonder, "Gee, how did I do that?"

Even at school, I would be daydreaming in search of answers. In reading groups, I would be distracted. Did Dick and Jane wonder why they were different from Spot? I listened attentively to my classmates to see if they had the same curiosity about their souls. I also paid close attention to adult conversations searching for tidbits of guidance. Possibly my grandparents knew the answers. They were certainly older and wiser than my twenty-something parents. I decided to approach my grandparents.

Even at this young age, I realized my dad's mom, Ga-Ga, would not be a likely candidate. She was not very approachable. I hated to kiss her because her breath always smelled like beer or whiskey, even in the morning. I wondered if maybe she did not feel comfort-able in her body, too. She did not appear to have the answers to any of my questions. My dad's father, Pop M, was one of the nicest people in the world. He always gave us ice cream and was a great cook—all qualities a kid could appreciate. I especially liked that he put his home-made chili on mashed potatoes. He would be a good candidate to ask, I thought.

One day, before I could muster my confidence up to ask him, I overheard a conversation about death in their living room. This would be a perfect opportunity to listen. I walked into the room acting disinterested in the topic at hand, waiting to hear the secret of life from my kind grandfather. I was shocked to hear the answer. We were worm bait—*plant food*. When we die, we are buried and there is nothing else. Just the deep-six, although I wasn't sure what that meant. I felt like screaming but held it in and walked out of the room. I went outside and went for a walk by myself down their suburban street. How could this be true? Is there no soul? No God? No something special about us? I thought about the possible truth of Pop's statements. If this were true, what a waste! I especially thought about Ga-Ga. She spent most of her time drinking and arguing with my grandfather, my mom, and my dad. Her own grandchildren didn't want to kiss her. How sad, I thought.

Anyway, I decided that I had plenty of time to live this life and would not waste it. Over time, I dismissed the statement of my paternal grandfather regarding *plant food*, nothingness after death, no separate soul. I began having the same feelings that had started my quest. An intense curiosity crept back into my consciousness. That desire to know we are souls, and that souls are separate from our bodies.

My search for the answer now focused on my mom's parents, Nan and Pop D. They were certainly the wisest people I knew. On many weekends, my parents would drop off my younger siblings and me at their house on Friday night and pick us up on Sunday afternoon.

Nan and Pop attended church on a regular basis. Some Sundays we went with them to church services. Many Sundays, Pop would stay home with us while Nan went to church alone. Looking back, I think he was giving Nan a break from having to dress three or four little kids, feed them breakfast, get them to church, keep them quiet in church, and return home to change into regular clothes before she prepared Sunday dinner. This was in addition to Nan's daily responsibility of taking care of Great-grandmother Schrauth. My great-grandmother, who was about ninety years old, also lived with my grandparents on Mitchell Avenue.

Nan and Pop were the central figures in raising us. I easily understood their religious beliefs. God exists. If you go to church, be a God-fearing person, treat people nicely, be respectful of adults, and help when you can, you will be granted the privilege of going to Heaven upon your death. These values were certainly closer to what I was feeling. Nan and Pop had faith that their religious values were true.

It was a struggle for me to figure out what faith meant. I was told faith was believing in something without proof of its existence. The examples of such a belief were God and Santa Claus. I was okay with the God example, but even at eight years old I was having my doubts about Santa Claus. I certainly couldn't share with my siblings, my parents, or friends that my *faith* did not extend to Santa Claus. Anyway, I was more interested in how faith in God worked.

During this time, I would watch television hoping to find the answer. Although I enjoyed watching TV, it was apparent that God's answer was not going to show up on *The Ed Sullivan Show*, *F-Troop*, *The Jetsons*, or *Lost in Space*. There was one program that held promise in my quest. Many Sunday mornings, I would wake up early before everyone else in the family and tune the television to *Davey & Goliath*. It was a religious Claymation cartoon about a boy named Davey and his dog Goliath. I felt a bond with Davey, not because we had the same name, but because he was on a search for answers, and I was on a search for answers. We even both had dogs, although his dog talked. The show was produced by the Evangelical Lutheran Church of America and first aired on January 1, 1961, with the episode "The Silver Mine." According to the series description on Amazon, "In each episode, Davey and Goliath experience some form of moral conflict either in themselves or in their friends. Drawing upon the guidance of his parents, his teachers, and his own religious beliefs, Davey doesn't always do the right thing, but he does always come away from the experience having learned valuable moral and life lessons." This show helped shape who I am today. It was my church.

Occasionally, my parents would bring us to the church down the road. I didn't mind going there. It was a friendly looking, small, white church with a tall steeple. I especially enjoyed that it was near the Dutchess County Airport, and during the services, I could hear planes taking off over the church. The sound of their propellers provided me with a welcome distraction from the sermon. I recall wondering if the pilot in the plane, who was enjoying a nice sunny day, blue skies, and a wonderful view of the green rolling hillsides, was closer to God than we were as we sat in the church listening to the minister. The minister had told us God created all the beauty in the world. I wondered why we were not outside enjoying nature.

I felt most people attended church because they believed it was the only place to get *in touch* with God. It puzzled me why adults felt they were not able to communicate with God in places other than at their church—like in their bedrooms or walking in the woods. I got the sense that most church attendees believed the ministers were *special* people who had this direct line to the Creator himself. The implication was that we did not have this ability to communicate with God, so the minister would do it on our behalf. Why was so much awe placed in the lap of the minister by the people attending? I also couldn't figure out why some people acted differently on Sundays, kind of nicer. Did they think God was only watching them on Sundays? Did they not know God was available on other days of the week? In other places? The more I attended church, the more questions I had about religion. It all was so confusing to me.

I dearly loved Nan and Pop, but attending church with them did not help me to answer my questions about religion. Nan and Pop's church was built around 1800 and was made of stone with a huge bell tower. It was beautiful in an awe-inspiring sort of way but felt cold, stuffy, and unfriendly to me. We were required to be on our best behavior while attending services. This was a struggle for my sisters and me, but out of respect for our grandparents, we all obliged. Sitting still, and not paying attention to the sermon, gave me plenty of time to contemplate. Plenty of time to watch people, too. The Harris' granddaughter had very pretty, blue eyes, I thought. Why did Ethyl always sit in the same pew wearing the same blue hat every Sunday? Why did Mr. Mitchell come to services when he always fell asleep? Such mysteries.

I wondered how God decided which church was more worthy. Was the old, awe-inspiring stone church with its massive bell tower and ornate stained-glass windows more worthy of His attention than the friendly-looking little white church by the airport that my parents had brought us to? I was certain religion had a place in God's plan, but at my age, I didn't understand what that place was. Each time I attended church my emotions would ride a roller coaster.

I wondered why there were so many religions. Why was Davey a Lutheran? Why were we Protestant? More specifically, what was a Dutch Reformed Protestant? How come my best friends were Catholic? Friends in school, along with my Aunt Roberta, were Jewish—what about them? How come some people hated other people just because of their religion? How come adults had made such a big deal about electing a Catholic president? Was he shot because he was the first Catholic president? More mysteries.

Even though I knew God loved and appreciated me, I felt inadequate to ask Him any questions. I did not want to anger him by being a pest. Therefore, many of these questions remained in my head. Occasionally, I asked my parents. They told me there were many different types of people and different ways to worship, none were better or worse than the other, just different. Their most important answer was that there was only one God. I believed that.

Most of the time, I took pleasure in the little things in life. I was happy I didn't have to dress up in a suit for Sunday service, and that Nan was going to cook pot roast for the Sunday dinner that followed church. The love between Nan and Pop, and their love for us, was enough to sustain me through those Sunday mornings.

Finally, I decided I needed proof my soul existed and was separate from my body. I felt I had exhausted all other ways of trying to get answers. I really truly wanted to have faith, but my curiosity was much stronger. So, one warm sunny summer day, I knew I could wait no longer to satisfy my quest. It was time. I decided to go straight to God to answer my question. I figured if Santa Claus knows when we are naughty and nice, certainly God knows the answers, too. I told my sisters not to come into the bedroom because I was going to take a nap. This was not necessarily a request that would arouse suspicion.

I went into my bedroom and closed the blinds to remove the distraction of the sunny day. I was nervous and apprehensive, as I had decided to go straight to the source—God—to prove I was more than just my physical body. This seemed the only logical way to get my answers. Now that the room was somewhat darkened, I pulled back my brown bed cover and laid down on my bed. I tried to get comfortable by fluffing the pillows, but it was really a stall tactic. I finally decided to lay on my back looking up at the ceiling.

Doubt and fear entered my mind. I thought, *I am only an eight-year-old kid. I don't pay attention when I go to church. There are billions of other people in the world, why would God have time to deal with me? What if God would become mad at my question? Would his punishment be worse than the belt, which was the punishment of choice when I was playing with matches last summer with my neighbor, Wayne? Or maybe my punishment would be eternal damnation, whatever that meant.*

I continued to lay still on my bed and could hear my siblings playing outside. They were having fun on this warm summer day, while I was in my room wondering how to ask God to resolve my dilemma. I wondered if they had these weird thoughts too. If they did, I could ask them to join me, and maybe I would be less afraid. I went through my memories to remember if they had ever wondered about life, about why we were here on Earth, about why we were born, about why we are different from animals, about where our feelings come from. Or whether they felt like a stranger in their own bodies. Nope. I guess I had to do this on my own.

My next thought was, *how do I ask God?* I was taught that God was in Heaven, up there, far away. It was logical that I was to yell as loud as I could. But would he think I was being disrespectful by yelling to him? My parents didn't like when we yelled at them. Besides, if I yelled, there was a possibility that someone else might hear me, then I would have some explaining to do. I scratched that plan and decided the quiet approach to God would have to do.

I finally set my fear aside and began speaking to God. Respect-fully, I asked for proof that I was correct in my belief there was something, maybe our soul, that something special that makes us who we are. I waited awhile and nothing at all happened. Since nothing had occurred after this initial inquiry, I decided I could relax. I politely repeated my desire to know. Gradually, I began to feel different. Like I was as light as a feather. I no longer was aware of my sisters playing in the yard. I was no longer aware of the mattress under my body. I felt like I was on a cloud, but was this the proof I was searching for?

At that moment, I turned around and saw myself lying on the bed! I was about six feet in the air looking at myself. In an instant of time, a millisecond, I was so joyful to know the answer. We do have souls and they exist separate from our bodies. Everything now made sense! But then, suddenly, an intense fear gripped me. I did not want to be separate from myself, and I was instantly back in my body staring at my bedroom ceiling. It was incredible! I knew I was right! I was so happy my question had been answered. Our souls DO exist separate from our physical bodies. I am my soul, not my body!

Then my thoughts started down a scary path. My soul had just separated from my body, did that mean I was dead? If I was dead, why was I still in my bedroom? I strained to hear the familiar sounds of my siblings playing outside but heard nothing. Was this God's punishment that I had heard about in church? Was I in Purgatory?

My heart raced with fear. My body felt like a thousand tons as I leapt from my bed. It felt like I was moving in slow motion as I threw open my bedroom door and rushed down the hallway looking for my parents or siblings. I called to my sisters. No one was there. Maybe they couldn't hear me because I was dead. I ran out the back door and saw my dad watering the garden. I ran up to him and said loudly, "Hi, Dad." He replied, "Hey, Dave, where have you been?" He sees me! I am not dead! I gave him a hug. He had no idea why.

A calm feeling finally came over me as I thought about the events that had occurred just moments before. The sunshine had a warmth on my skin I had never appreciated before. The freshly mown grass smelled especially good. I felt more alive than ever. Silently, I thanked God for answering my question. I thanked Him that I was alive. I now knew who I was. I went to play baseball.

A Spiritual Perspective on Soul-based Identity

At the time

My memory of this experience was that I was floating in the air looking down at my own body. I had no recollection of my physical body looking up and seeing my soul floating. Only the memory of me—*my soul*—looking down at my body. At eight years old, I knew that I was a soul—inside a body.

This awareness helped me deal with my own physical insecurity—*big ears*. Other kids would call me "Dumbo" and flick my ears from behind my back. I would get on the school bus and find a seat in front of the kids I knew would not flick my ears on the way to school. I relay this story because everyone has physical attributes that they are uncomfortable with, or they feel uncomfortable in their body. We judge ourselves. We create insecurities about our bodies that can manifest into many different realities and can morph into making judgments of others just to make ourselves feel better.

One time, after relaying certain kids (especially Joe) were bullying me on the bus about my ears, I overheard my parents discussing the possibility of surgery to correct my protruding ears. They had decided not to proceed, and I was mad about that for a long while. When I finally confronted them about it, they simply said, "When you are old enough to make a mature decision about this, you may decide on your own how to surgically alter your body." My only reply was, "How old is that?" Their response was, "When you are eighteen." That seemed so far away. Eventually, I let go of my anger. I understood that I was soul energy inside this body. It made me more comfortable in my own skin. I was glad my parents, unknowingly, had allowed my awakening to continue. And that they didn't let an eight-year-old dictate a bodily change that would impact me for the rest of my life.

Throughout my youth, I never really understood why there were so many different religions and why people were so protective of their specific way of worshipping God. I ignored any discussion about how one religion was better than another but was quite interested in the special ceremonies my friends were experiencing in their religions, partially for my own understanding and partially to ensure I wasn't missing some important lesson.

For example, when Paul and Mike made their first Communion, we walked across the street to congratulate them and see them in their bright white robes. When my school friend, John, was celebrating Yom Kippur, I was quite interested in the meaning of his celebration—curious enough to sit with him during lunch even though he was eating a smelly limburger cheese sandwich! Even Easter held such a great opportunity to have discussions with adults about the significance of this Christian holiday. Despite my curiosity regarding religious ceremonies, I was certain in my belief God was available to everyone, regardless of their families' religious upbringing. I knew everyone was really a soul inside their body. A simple truth that has guided my life experiences.

As I write today

In our society, it is an incredibly difficult concept to accept—to be comfortable in one's own skin. All children should be taught they are God's children—each made differently—each made perfectly. Loving and respecting these differences is what makes us stronger as human beings.

For a moment, accept the concept that we are beings of light having a physical experience within this time-space dimension. It would be a nicer world if we could see what's on the inside instead of judging what's on the outside. I think Martin Luther King said it best, "I have a dream that my four little children will one day live in a nation where they will not be judged by the color of their skin but by the content of their character."

We have forgotten, or learned to avoid, the conscious effort to see below skin deep. We have been coerced by those controlling the message into believing prejudiced generalizations and agendas that purposely create racial animosity. By judging a person on their physical appearance, we have become separated and blinded to their soul. We have become what I call a *soul-blind* society.

Can we just be like Crayola Crayons? The first box of Crayola Crayons was produced in 1903 as an eight-count box. It only contained the colors red, orange, yellow, green, blue, violet, brown, and black. Now you can buy a pack of crayons with 124 different shades—all existing together in one package! Crayola has not succumbed to the "separation-by-race" culture where skin color matters. In fact, Crayola is just the opposite. They recognize that we are ALL people of color. As of this writing, they still sell a package of twenty-four crayons, called *Colors of the World*, representing that God-created a diversity of skin tones throughout humanity. All inclusive. All shades of white, pink, yellow, tan, and brown. Kudos to Crayola.

I have also witnessed separation and soul blindness within structured religion. I think everyone has heard the religious joke that goes something like this:

> *A man passes away and finds himself at St. Peter's gate. After the obligatory life review by St. Peter, the man is granted entrance to Heaven. Upon entering, the man asks, "Where shall I go now? Who should I see?" St. Peter offers up a kind response, "Well, I'm not that busy so let me show you around." As the tour progresses, the man feels very blessed to be in such a beautiful setting. He only has one perplexing question, "Why is there a large wall over there that seems to go on forever?" St. Peter replies, "Oh, the wall. Yes, on the other side are the* [insert religion here]. *They think they are the only ones in Heaven!"*

I have seen this "joke" told by different religious people mocking other religions as invalid, or not allowed into Heaven, or those *other* people are going to Hell. Why? They are soul blind, too. Creating separation in the name of Jesus. It's hard for me to believe that some religious people are soul blind to that extent, or soul blind at all.

How do you recognize soul blindness? It is a focus on a particular physical, religious, or political characteristic that blinds the observer to the true nature of all humans as light-filled souls. Soul blindness can easily be used as a control mechanism—to create separation based upon skin color, religious beliefs, political beliefs, or a whole variety of other physical or cultural attributes—ignoring that we are all God's children equal in His eyes.

But how did we get here? We are constantly bombarded with body-image propaganda. We have become unaware that our physical appearance, insecurities, and self-judgments have been used to sell beauty products, pharmaceuticals, and gadgets just to increase corporate profits. Not that I'm against companies being profitable, but these companies seem to base their products and profits on our compliance to judge, not only ourselves, but others, too. As a society, we have become body-centric and soul blind.

My personal favorites are the advertisements for baldness prevention products, promoted as if a lack of hair is a social disease. As I see these advertisements and social media postings, they grant me the opportunity to thank God for my beautiful, shiny head. I thank Him for the opportunity to rise above self-judgment and to be comfortable in my own skin. I have even made friends with my ears!

Finding Clarity:
Am I able to love others and recognize that they are perfect children of God?

I can tell you this, God's love rises above our mortal voices. His love rises above those who would create soul blindness in our society. Just like my eight-year-old self, reach out to communicate with God—or use alternative thoughts that make you comfortable —Jesus, or the Universal energy. We are all connected to *it*. Through our dreams, through the small, still voice within our hearts, through music, through chance meetings on the street. We must learn to listen—to become aware of these Universal energies. God also speaks to us through guardian angels—more on that later.

The search to experience love—love of oneself and love of others—is our soul work. For some people, organized religion is the perfect framework for their soul work—their path to define love. Structured religion also has a place in our world because there are many paths to God. The key factor in its success or failure resides within each individual soul searching for a closer relationship with God—an enhanced experience of love.

As my life's soul work has progressed, I have searched for my place in the religious structure of our world in many different places and in many ways. I was born into a Protestant family. In my life, I have studied *Course in Miracles*, experienced years of study under a brilliant teacher with his Doctorate in Metaphysical Studies, and spent years reading the *Book of Morman*, including the *Doctrine and Covenants* and *The Pearl of Great Price*. I was a member of the National Spiritualist Association of Churches (NSAC). I have been blessed to take deep, life meaning from each of these experiences.

I have also been surrounded by friends and loved ones who searched in their own ways. My first wife was Jewish. My former sister-in-law was raised Jewish but follows the structure of Shamanism. My former brother-in-law was raised Jewish but follows the structure of Christianity. My granddaughters are Catholic. My brother-in-law espouses to be atheist. My cousin is a youth minister in a Southern Baptist Church. My sister has been honored by a tribal elder in an Ojibwa naming ceremony also honoring Giitchi Manidoo, the Ojibwa great god. My wife practiced Catholicism. All are just labels for our individual connection to God, and to our true inner selves.

Each path potentially takes us individually toward the discovery that God is there and has always been there, waiting to receive us—in life and in death. If your present religious journey does not touch your heart, give you joy, or surround you in love, then choose a new direction. He provides many paths. If your path is guided by love, then revel in your own personal unique journey.

My spiritual journey began during a life crisis, not unlike most people's awakenings. As I sat alone at the small table reserved for coffee lovers—like myself—just outside the Caribou Coffee Kiosk inside Tower City in Cleveland, Ohio, I was attracted to the bookstore across the mall area. *Maybe I could find a book that would help me,* I thought. I decided to check it out after my counseling session. This was the third or fourth time during my first marriage that I had been in counseling, either alone or together, it was hard to remember. All I knew was that something was missing and maybe a book would help—maybe even reading the Bible. I wondered if that bookstore had a Bible in stock.

"Do you carry Bibles in this bookstore?" I inquired with the young man at the front cash register. Umm, sure, I think aisle six or seven on the right, he stated as if he had never been asked that question before. Excitedly, I found the Bibles in aisle seven on the right. My excitement turned to confusion, as I realized there were two whole shelves of different Bibles. At forty years old, I felt like that little kid sitting in church confused about religion. Which Bible should I choose? The *King James Version*, the *New International Version (NIV)*, the *New American Bible*, the *New King James Version* were only a few of the daunting choices. I decided to pray. I closed my eyes. "*Dear Lord, I am very confused. Please show me any type of sign that will help me find the perfect book to read at this time in my life. Amen."*

As I opened my eyes, a bright white light emanated from a book on the lowest shelf, a place I hadn't looked before. I smiled and reached down for whatever Bible I was to read. The book was *Conversations with God: An Uncommon Dialogue, book 1* by Neale Donald Walsch. The inside jacket said, "Suppose you could ask God the most puzzling questions about existence – questions about love and faith, life and death, good and evil. Suppose God provided clear, understandable answers." Yes! Thank you, God. I know this is the right book for me because twenty-five years earlier while sitting on a log in Wilcox Park, I had the very same experience! I had experienced my own conversation with God, as detailed in a later chapter in this book. My prayer had been answered. I knew I had just begun the next part of my spiritual journey. I felt it in my heart.

The mere fact you are reading this now makes this moment the next step of your own journey. God hears your heart and knows your soul. See the soul's light inside of people who are different from you. And know God is right next to you. He is waiting for you to talk to Him. I was blessed to learn this lesson when I was just eight years old.

Daily Affirmation

I will see the light in everyone I meet.

"A miracle is never lost. It may touch many people you have not even met and produce undreamed of changes in situations of which you are not even aware."

~ *A Course in Miracles*, Chapter 1(I) Paragraph 45*

* This quote is from *A Course in Miracles*, copyright ©1992, 1999, 2007 by the Foundation for Inner Peace, 448 Ignacio Blvd., #306, Novato, CA 94949, *www.acim.org*, used with permission.

Chapter Two

My Fourth Grade Teacher

A Spiritual Perspective on Miracles

Miracles Await You

David K. Munson ©2020

Your sadness hides behind brown eyes.
A smile abandons your face –
beautiful potential.

Your soul hides behind a disguise.
Lightness abandons your heart –
beautiful potential.

Your spirit hides behind a struggle.
A miracle of love awaits –
To awaken your beautiful potential.

As I went through my ninth and tenth years on this planet, I was comforted to know God was available. I figured if He was available to an eight-year-old kid in a green farmhouse in Red Oaks Mill, He must be available to everyone. All you needed to do was ask, although I figured the question better be very important.

I was still fully engaged with my struggle to understand the world and religion. My thoughts wandered. In school, I spent countless hours observing the interactions among my classmates. I didn't have many friends in school. Maybe there was some quality I was lacking. To top it off, I struggled in all school subjects.

I knew I was really my soul, not just my body. This made me hurt even more when other kids teased me about my big ears. Didn't they understand there was more to me than that? *Dumbo* was not my favorite Disney movie. All I saw was when Dumbo was being relentlessly teased. I was not ready to see when he used his God-given gifts to fly! I preferred *The Sword in the Stone*, where a poor rag-tag servant boy was misjudged and mistreated—only to discover his true self was destined to become a humble king.

Teachers have a special place on God's Earth guiding His children. It is a great responsibility. My fourth-grade teacher had an important impact on my early life. I will not mention her name in this text. At the right time, God will guide her here to read this, and she will recognize herself in this miracle. Or I will see her in the hereafter. Allow me to tell my story.

The Dutchess County Fair was over, the one sure sign that summer was coming to its rapid conclusion. I dreaded going back to school. My annual struggle shopping for new clothes was finally over. I'm sure my mom thought it was a boy thing, not wanting to go shopping for clothes. For me, it was a struggle to find a balance between buying clothes that were in style and finding clothes that would not make me stand out. The less kids noticed me, the less teasing I would get about my ears. I would choose the stylish clothes in drab colors of brown or green as we shopped for our wardrobe at the Rhinebeck Thrift Shop or the church's Nearly New Shoppe where Nan volunteered each week. At least those places weren't in my school district, so the chances of running into a classmate was low. I didn't want them to find out my "new" school clothes were from second-hand shops.

On the first day of fourth grade, I was nervous to be going to a different elementary school. I wasn't even sure where Fishkill Plains Elementary School was located. The bus ride seemed long. When we arrived, I was happy to see my teacher was young. Up until now, all my former teachers had been old—close to retirement. My new teacher had just gotten married that past summer, so her name was different than we had expected. She was pretty and had a lot of energy. Discussion groups, talking in front of the class, constant desk rearrangement, and her positive reinforcement all enticed me to become involved in school. The more I tried to blend into the woodwork, the more she would not let me.

I remember how scared I was the time she paired us in teams of two to give a science presentation to the class. She assigned me with Keith, one of my new friends. That was a relief, although our topic was about how we hear. I was devastated to think I had to stand up in front of the whole class and focus on hearing—my ears! Keith and I worked on our class presentation, and I learned there was more to the inside of our ears than you could see from the outside. What's inside was *more* important. I understood that concept! I always wondered if that was my teacher's intention. As a note of fate— *because there is no such thing as a coincidence* —eight years later, Keith was my college freshman roommate. We both studied science —and he became a doctor!

Finally, I felt part of the class, rather than an outsider. I discovered I could have friendships in school without judgment or teasing. I realized I was smarter than I thought, and I began to enjoy what we were learning. My religious contemplations were relegated to weekends. I no longer merely observed my classmates' inter-actions, I became actively involved in relationships. Our teacher treated us like people and involved us in her experience of being pregnant.

One day, in the spring of 1966, she did not show up to school. Our substitute did not know why she was not there, only saying that she was ill. The principal came to our class, which was never a good sign, to explain that our teacher had lost her baby. A miscarriage. I felt tremendous sadness. Tears welled up in my eyes and I had a lump in my throat. I wanted to ask God why. I did not lift my head to look around at my classmates. I was afraid they would see the tears rushing to my eyes. The teasing would start again, and all the good school feelings would go away. I raised my hand with one finger up, the universal sign that I had to go to the bathroom. I hurried out of the classroom and ran down the hall to the bathroom. I cried by myself, as quiet as I could be.

The weeks she was not there seemed to drag. While she was gone, I missed her special gift of teaching, being with kids, helping us grow. I wondered if God didn't think she would be a wonderful mother. It was clear to me there were many mysteries that still needed to be solved. I was worried about the day my teacher would return to school. My heart was still sad about her loss. I knew that when I saw her, I would want to run up, give her a hug, and tell her we loved her. I might cry. I knew I couldn't do that, so I prepared for a difficult emotional day.

Finally, she was back. At my first glance, I could see in her eyes that her heart was sad. Unfortunately, within the first five minutes, someone in class raised their hand and asked why she lost her baby. Tears welled up in her eyes and she went into the hallway. I could not believe it. How could he be so insensitive to her feelings! My disbelief quickly turned to anger, and I could not sit by and allow this to happen. I mustered every ounce of courage I had hoping to set aside the years of fear about being different. For the first time in my life, I stood up in class and shouted at my classmate, "She is still sad about losing her baby. We should not ask her stupid questions about it! She will tell us when she is ready. It is our job to be good students and make sure she knows we are happy that she is back and that she is *our* teacher." I sat down. My whole body was shaking, and my heart was pounding. I did not care about what my classmates thought about me. I was proud of myself. I would take the teasing the rest of the year if I could help my favorite teacher get through her sadness.

In time, things settled down, back to normal. The teasing, which I expected over my outburst in class, never occurred. The class rallied to show her how much we appreciated her. I was happy the thoughts and feelings I had in my heart came out in a way that helped her. I went about enjoying the rest of that school year. I was never sure if my teacher knew about that day when I stood up in class in her defense. It didn't really matter because I knew. And God knew.

On my final fourth grade report card, I was proud that, for the first time in school, I had gotten straight A grades. More importantly, she had written something special, "David has a happy personality. He is very much aware of the feelings of others. His understanding and feelings for others are well developed and mature." I was a better person because she took the time to reach me, touch my heart, and change my life. A miracle of love.

A Spiritual Perspective on Miracles

At the time

I was not equipped to view this situation—my growth—through any other lens than that of a shy fourth grader. I knew the depth of my emotions and understanding of others' feelings seemed deeper than my peers. And I sure didn't know what to do with that. Ultimately, I went into fifth grade confident that everything would be alright.

As I write today

As I look back on this period of my life, I had not previously appreciated the depth of my change in fourth grade. In my introduction to this chapter, I noted this story as a miracle. As I first did, some of you could view this as an exaggeration of the word miracle. My experience in fourth grade did not include angels. There were no visions from the heavens, and no voices from God or deceased loved ones (*those stories are later in this book*). On the surface, my experience seemed like the normal growth of a confused, shy boy who was guided by the dedication and love of a teacher—and that's exactly what it was, a miracle of the heart.

Miracles occur every day in a million different ways. According to *A Course in Miracles*, Chapter 1(I), Paragraph 3; "Miracles occur naturally as expressions of love. The real miracle is the love that inspires them. In this sense *everything* that comes from love is a miracle."

When you act from a place of love, you create a ripple effect through the infinite energy that freely flows through and beyond time and space. Your ripple effect moves through a sea of vibrational energy to which we are all connected—to create miracles of love for others. We may be totally unaware of the positive effects our actions create. And these ripples exist at such a high vibrational level, they can be felt over many lifetimes or impact generations to come.

Nearly fifty years later, I became a first-time teacher. I taught high school chemistry, middle school STEM (science, technology, engineering, and math), and high school engineering in Arizona. I loved teaching and interacting with my students. I always tried to interact in a manner that reflected understanding, respect, and love for my students. Just as my fourth-grade teacher had helped me, I tried to pass that along to another generation.

In the spring of 2015, one of my Honors STEM class students approached me after class with the statement, "I have something important to tell you, and I know you will keep it in confidence." I answered, "Yes, as long as it doesn't endanger you or another student, I will keep your confidence." She began cautiously, "Well, I think I'm a lesbian and I haven't told anyone else. What should I do?" With my teacher hat, I replied, "If you feel you need to discuss this with a professional, the school has a counselor, and it will be confidential." As she shrugged her shoulders, she said, "No, I'm just not sure right now."

I spoke from my heart, "It's okay to be gay. And it's also okay to be unsure. You're only in middle school, and you have a lot of time to decipher your feelings. Just remember that you are not defined by that. You are a smart girl, and a very talented artist. You have time to explore all your talents and feelings. There's no rush. That's what the next few years are for—to grow into who you really are. No self-judgment. And when the time is right, you should sit down with your parents and discuss this with them. They are your greatest advocates. In the meanwhile, my lips are sealed." As we ended the conversation, she said, "I knew you would give me good advice, thank you."

Finding Clarity:
Am I able to be aware of all influences impacting my child's development and safety?

This example points out one thing I feel strongly about—parents need to be involved in their child's social, emotional, and intellectual development. They need to be aware and play an active role. This includes researching their child's school curriculum and teachers. Parents must not depend on others to nurture their children's growth. In our world today, others may have social, sexual, religious, political, victimhood/oppressor, or personal agendas inconsistent with your own family values. Enough about that.

Many times, we are unaware of the ripples we create that make an impact on others. After three years of teaching, I retired into another career and received this letter from one of my students:

Dear Mr. Munson,

Normally, I am a solid writer, and my strongest quality is always my opening sentences. However, when I opened this document to write this letter, so many things flooded into my head, and it put me at a loss. I was devastated when you told us all that you would be moving, and I wanted to say good-bye and write you this letter to really thank you, and so you have something to remember me by. When we first met at the beginning of my eighth-grade year, I was drowning in my teenage rebellion punk phase. Most people would have looked at me and thought I was purely the punk "I don't care" attitude I put out for people to see. But you, you looked at me and saw potential. I voiced my interest in engineering and the world, and you didn't let me push it aside. You helped me realize that being smart isn't a bad thing, and that I have so much more potential than I thought. As I grew and matured, and finally realized the catastrophe that was my emo phase, you taught me to believe in myself. The lessons you have taught me are those that you could find in no textbook. You have always been way more to me than just a teacher, you've been a role model. The care and dedication you showed me, and your students, is amazing and something to look up to. My diseases and problems always seem an easy thing to overcome thanks to you. You're always ready to offer advice and a helping hand. Because of you, I know that I should never give up on myself or doubt my abilities. You've also shown me that I shouldn't doubt others, because everyone has something to offer, and everyone has amazing potential. When I'm around you, I want to learn, and you emit a vibe of safety and light. When I'm around you, I'm on the same level as all my peers, and it's a wonderful learning environment. I am forever grateful to you because you've had an effect on me that will last forever. I truly believe I am a better person thanks to you, and I will miss you dearly. I'll forever remember my eighth grade STEM teacher who believed in me. I will continue to believe in myself and always do my best and help people. I'm going to miss you a ton and I wish you the best.

Sincerely, J.

I pray that every teacher has a letter like this stashed in their desk. Miracles are sown by acts of love ruled by our heart and weave their energy ripples through the time and space of human existence. I hope my fourth-grade teacher would be proud of me.

Daily Affirmation

Thank you for opening my heart to create
a miracle in someone's life.

"Greater than fear is love. Love dissolves all fear, casts out all doubt and sets the captive free."
~ **Ernest Holmes,** *The Science of Mind*

Chapter Three

A Yellow Rocking Chair

A Spiritual Perspective on Unconditional Love

Thoughts Aren't Deeds

David K. Munson ©2021

Naughts aren't ney,
and needs aren't hay.
And in the dense,
curds aren't whey
.

When thoughts in the gray
aren't voiced in the fray,
Acts of love
are kept at bay.

A present given today,
the gift to kneel and pray.
Your deeds are now done,
and come what may.

Our family had a routine almost every Saturday as my sisters Karen and Sue, cousin Jack, and I invaded Nan and Pop's house on Mitchell Avenue to spend the night. It was not lost on me that we were being dumped-off by our young twenty-something parents so they could go out with friends and party. It didn't matter. For me, it was the only place on Earth where I could just be a kid, without worrying about taking care of my younger sisters and cousin. I knew they loved us. They were our grandparents. They were adults! I could just be myself with them.

As we arrived each Saturday, I would run inside to give Nan a hug, then head straight for the freezer to determine what flavor Breyers ice cream I would be enjoying after dinner. Then off to the little wooden box that hung on the dining room wall to see what flavor Wrigley's gum was inside—spearmint or wintergreen. And then a beeline for the living room, where an antique candy dish always had something in it—M&M's, gumdrops (the spice kind), Turkish taffy, Good & Plenty licorice, or butterscotch buttons. Something different every week!

Following our hunt for candy, Nan would tell us what project Pop was working on and to stay out of the way. Of course, for me, it was an open invitation to go check it out. But before that, there was always the reminder, "Put your bags in the guest room and don't forget to hug your great-grandmother!"

Great-grandma Schrauth was the oldest person I knew. My great-grandmother was a proud German woman, always dignified in manner. For my whole life, she had lived with Nan and Pop in the extra bedroom. Her knees could no longer support her sturdy, big-boned frame, so she spent most days sitting in her yellow-cushioned rocking chair looking out the window into the backyard. Their backyard was beautiful—full of award-winning rose bushes of every color and hue. Pop was a master rose gardener. There were also bird feeders, a thirty-foot fishpond with pink and yellow blooming lily pads, Koi fish, and a four-foot green copper fountain of a nearly naked boy spitting water through a conch shell into the fishpond. It was a unique backyard, to say the least.

Inside, Great-grandma's bedroom had just enough room for two twin beds with old-fashioned white comforter blankets, a dresser with lace doilies, a black and white television, her brass bell, and a TV tray that held her meals. Although I never gave it much thought, I imagine every morning started with Nan (her daughter) getting her out of bed, getting her to the bathroom, washing up, getting her dressed into her navy-blue dress with the small white polka dots, and into her special, yellow-cushioned rocking chair. Last, but not least, neatly making her bed without a wrinkle.

Since Great-grandma could not walk, she had a big brass bell, and it was never far from her reach. She would ring it if she needed something. "Go see what your great-grandma wants," Nan would say to us. There were typically four reasons she rang the bell: she needed help to go to the bathroom; she would request something to drink; she would ask us to change the channel on the TV; or she would scold us for something we were doing earlier in the day. You see, we knew Great-grandma was watching us through her window as we played in the backyard. Most of the time, we would just wave and go along our way.

Other times, we would purposely be mischievous just to see how long it took for her to knock on the window and shake her finger in disapproval. Let me be clear in admitting I was usually the instigator of the mischief. My cousin and I would: stage a fake fight in the grass; stand on the edge of the fishpond pretending to lose our balance about to fall into the water; start to climb the maple tree in the backyard; balance on the rock garden wall where my grandfather's award-winning roses were growing; and last but not least, pretend to pick our noses by holding our fingers next to our nose. My creativity for mischief held no bounds—although my favorite pastime was a simple game of catch with my cousin. If we made a bad throw or missed the baseball, it would end up in either the fishpond or a bed of thorny rose bushes. It was pressure-packed, and this yard honed our baseball skills.

When it was raining, we would create mischief inside. Our favorite game was to quietly slide on the wooden oak floor into Great-grandma Schrauth's bedroom and hide under the double set of twin beds while she sat in her yellow rocker. Sometimes, Nan would catch us and give us a dust rag to catch "dust bunnies" under the beds. Most of the time, Great-grandma would hear us and declare, "I know you're under there, you little rascals." We would laugh and be on our way to another adventure at Nan and Pop's house.

The evenings were always relaxing and quiet while we watched Saturday night television. We knew eating ice cream would be involved, and I always knew which Breyers flavors were in the freezer. Ice cream was in the Schrauth genes, and by default, mine!

[In 1865, Jacob Schrauth opened Schrauth Bakery in Poughkeepsie, NY. His inspiration was "the rich should not be the only ones to enjoy this delicacy. Let's bring ice cream to the common people." Their store at 151 Main Street was in the perfect location. Hudson River steamboats would always stop in Poughkeepsie, the halfway point in their journey between New York City and Albany, the capital of New York State. Travelers would walk up the hill from the boat docks on the Hudson River to enjoy a pastry or ice cream in the booming post-Civil War northern economy.

A few years back I had watched a show about the history of ice cream shops in America. It credited a family in Philadelphia with opening the first ice cream shop in 1865, although they stirred the ice cream with a mule in the backyard and sold the ice cream off their porch. I think the show did not do enough research.

Jacob Schrauth opened a real storefront ice cream shop in Poughkeepsie, NY in the same year—without mules!]

Going to Nan and Pop's almost every weekend gave us stability. After evening ice cream and some television—typically *The Lawrence Welk Show*—Nan would announce it was time for bed. On cue, all four of us kids would protest and ask for one more show. Looking back, I think it was Nan's strategy because she always easily relented, "OK, just one more show." Pop would peer over the rim of his reading glasses to watch this weekly ritual. He never said a word. He went back to studying the stock market in *The Wall Street Journal*. He didn't mind if we were up a little longer.

When it was time, we would all go quietly up the three stairs into the hallway past Great-grandma's bedroom. She had gone to sleep much earlier in the evening. I am sure she was exhausted from knocking on the window all day! Our bedroom was just big enough to fit two twin beds and two cots—the door barely closed. We would keep track of whose turn it was, boys or girls, to sleep in the beds or, should I say, not on the cots. Every weekend—I mean every weekend—Nan would declare, "Whoever gets to sleep first will get a nickel in the morning!" Every weekend—I mean every weekend—we would all fake snore to indicate who deserved the nickel. Funny thing, Nan gave each of us a nickel in the morning. Every weekend.

Then one weekend, it happened. Inconsistency. We had arrived at Nan and Pop's, and I jumped up the three stairs into the hallway to go say hi and hug Great-grandma Schrauth, but she was not there. I turned to see if the bathroom door was closed. Not there either. I ran downstairs and asked Mom, "Where is Great-grandma?"

"She was not feeling well, so she is in a special hospital for older people who are ill," my mom stated in such an upbeat way as to completely arouse my suspicions as to how serious this situation really was. I nonchalantly hung around the adults for a little while to see if I could hear a tidbit or two about the real story.

After Karen, Sue, and Jack were busy with other things, I approached my mom and whispered, "Is Great-grandma going to die?" I didn't want Nan to hear my question. I wasn't even sure if ten-year old kids were supposed to even ask those questions. "I don't know," she replied. I knew she was telling the truth. I heard it in her voice. She didn't even seem upset I had asked. So, I decided to take it one step further. "Then I want to go see her!" I announced. "No, that is not possible," she replied. Then I knew it was probably bad. Great-grandma was sicker than any of the adults were telling us kids. I snuck upstairs and did something I had NEVER done in my life—I sat in Great-grandma's yellow rocking chair. It felt strange. I looked out the window and saw my sisters and cousin playing in the yard. I leaned forward and lightly knocked on her window.

The next few weeks were very hard. It was only two years earlier I had laid on my bed at home and asked God about whether our souls were separate from our bodies. During that experience my soul left my body, so I knew Great-grandma's soul would still exist after her body died. That thought gave me much peace . . . and much fear.

Every night, I said a prayer hoping Great-grandma Schrauth would not die at night. During the day while I was in school—okay—but please God, don't let her die at night. I was so scared I might wake up and she would be standing at the bottom of my bed. During those weeks, the cars passing by on New Hackensack Road made unusual lights and shadows on my bedroom ceiling and walls that activated my frightened imagination. I was sure I saw her face looking in my bedroom window many times. Each morning I would ask Mom, "Do you think Great-grandma is coming home today?" I was always hopeful the answer might be yes, but it was really my way of asking, "Did she pass away last night?"

I truly do not remember what time of day she passed away, but she did not come to my bed to say good-bye, that I know of. I was sad we had not been able to say good-bye in person while she was still alive. It had all seemed so abrupt. As usual, I stuck close to the adult conversations maybe to hear insights or conversations they may have about death and dying. All I heard were funeral arrangements. No insights. The most troubling of those arrangements was that the great-grandkids were not going to the funeral. I could not believe what I was hearing!

Since I already knew souls exist outside the body, I was certain she would be at her own funeral. I *had* to go because I knew she would be there. I wanted to say good-bye to her. I wanted to tell her I loved her. It did not seem as frightening as lying in my bed at night in the dark, all alone. I would be with other people at her funeral—but with my own gigantic secret. When I said good-bye, she would hear me. I just knew it.

How would a ten-year-old convince adults to change their minds while they were so engrossed in funeral arrangements? I needed reinforcements—my sisters and cousin. I would have to convince them it was important to be there—to see her one last time. My plan was to show a unified front—all four of us kids really, really wanted to say good-bye. It was the truth.

Mom was sad at the loss of her grandmother, so I took a low-key approach. "Please think about letting us go to the funeral. We all want to go. Right, guys," I stated and looked at them so they would nod on cue. "And we promise to be good. Right, guys?" I had to choose my words carefully, but all I wanted to do was blurt, "Great-grandma will be there, so I want to be there with her!" My mom responded with, "Okay, I'll talk to your dad when he gets home." Perfect, I thought. I knew my mom was in no emotional position to make this decision, or to fight on our behalf, but if convinced, Dad would go the distance against tradition. I'm not sure about the difficulty of that task, but he successfully convinced the elders that the great-grandchildren should attend. Looking back, it was probably a big limb for my dad to go out on, two ten-year-old boys and two even younger girls at a funeral. It just wasn't done in those days.

Funny thing, I only remember two things from the funeral. I took personal responsibility for making sure the four of us kids upheld our promise to be good. It was important we show the elders that our parents' trust in us was not misplaced. I clearly remember seeing Great-grandma Schrauth looking so peaceful in her casket and knowing it was not really her, but only her body. I whispered that I missed her and knew she must have heard me. Good-byes are important.

After missing a day of school for the funeral, I easily got back into the routine at home. I no longer felt Great-grandma would come to my bedside at night to say good-bye. Good-byes were said at the funeral. My parents gave Nan and Pop a few weeks off from having us sleep over. It made sense to me. They needed time to adjust. It seemed so odd being in my own bed on a Saturday night.

After three weeks, it was finally the weekend we would go back to Nan and Pop's house. I had missed it—going for a walk down the street to Ethyl's house, stopping at the old red brick school playground to swing, and a final stop at the little store with the green Breyers leaf sign squeaking as the wind rocked it back and forth.

Oh, who is Ethyl? She was one of Nan's best friends, lived just a block or two away, and was always the first stop on our walks.

I loved that routine. I loved running ahead so I could be the first one to knock on her back door. Nan would yell, "David, you get back here. Wait for us!" Compared to Nan, Ethyl was a petite woman, but they both had big hearts. Ethyl would always act surprised to see us, and with a big smile she would give us a candy and a hug. She would always say how big we were getting—even if we had seen her just the Saturday before. We didn't ever stay long, because there were swings ahead and the store with the Breyers green leaf sign where we could spend our nickel on a vanilla/chocolate Dixie cup with the wooden spoon. I wondered if Nan would be in the mood for a walk this weekend.

As we arrived at Nan and Pop's, Nan greeted us with her usual big hug. When Nan hugged you, you knew you were being hugged. It was full of love. We all ran up the three stairs to put our stuff in the back guest bedroom. It had already been discussed in the car on the way that it was the girls turn to have the beds—the two of us boys would be on the cots. Oh well, it was our turn anyway.

As we ran through the bedroom door to throw our overnight bags onto the two beds and two cots, we were shocked to see the cots were not set up in the guest room, only the two beds. The girls jumped on and claimed the beds. They were already giggling and smiling at their good fortune, as my cousin and I looked at each other with puzzled faces. Where were we sleeping?

We immediately dashed back down the hallway and jumped into the living room not even touching any of the three steps. My mom hadn't left yet and was talking with Nan, probably seeing how she was doing over the past couple of weeks since Great-grandma had passed away. My cousin and I interrupted, "The cots are not set up. Where are we going to sleep?" My greatest fear was realized when Nan said, "You are sleeping in Great-grandma's bedroom."

"NO! We don't want to," we both screamed in unison. I tried to soften our reaction by pretending we really liked sleeping on the cots. Again, I tried to soften our reaction by saying the girls would miss us, but none of that was helping. We would just have to resort to the whining, "But why? Why do we have to sleep in Great-grandma's bedroom? We don't want to!"

Mom was trying her best to calmly reason with us. Smack in the middle of our on-going whining and ranting, I caught a glimpse of Nan's face. Her eyes were tearing up. She looked so sad. And I knew we were the cause. Instantly, I stopped mid-sentence and pulled my cousin into the next room for a cousin-to-cousin talk. I am certain he thought we were going to discuss our next strategy for ensuring we would sleep on the cots tonight. Instead, I said, "We are the boys. We are the oldest in the family. We must sleep in Great-grandma's bedroom." With Jack's reaction, I knew this was going to be a tough negotiation.

What I wanted to say was, "I know Great-grandma's soul still exists outside of her body, and she could be in her bedroom tonight with us. But we still need to do this anyway and be brave because Nan is very sad." Instead, I said, "We only must do it tonight, next week will be the girls' turn. Besides, we are the oldest. We must step up." Jack was not yet convinced, so for Nan's sake, I had to make one of the scariest commitments I had ever made in my ten years of life. I said, "OK. Here's the deal. I'll sleep in Great-grandma's bed, you can sleep in the other bed she never used—BUT you must stay awake until I fall asleep." I was so scared I would see Great-grandma's ghost in her very own bedroom. I figured if Jack stayed awake until I fell asleep, then I would make it through the night until morning. That was my strategy anyway. Jack reluctantly agreed. We returned to where Mom and Nan were still talking, and I happily informed them we would sleep in Great-grandma's bedroom. Nan's face lit up instantly. She gave us the biggest, biggest hugs. I felt this was special. It was the right thing to do. I was so totally scared.

I really don't recall the rest of the day's activities. I was probably consumed with trying to forget about bedtime, although bedtime came anyway. Our plea for an extra show brought us the typical half-hour bedtime delay, but on this occasion, I was not as happy about it as the others. To delay longer, I would have to be more creative than ever. I could fake being sick, although it had a potentially negative consequence of being sent to bed even earlier. I was going to try this tactic: *We're older than the girls, and now that we are in separate rooms, it only seems right the boys get another extra half-hour to stay up.* It seemed like a Hail Mary! Nan's expression implied she would consider it. I knew this had to do with whether it was okay with Pop if we stayed up later than ever before. I glanced in his direction for any indication or hint about this critical decision. He looked at me, smiled, and winked. I think he really appreciated my negotiating skills.

But the extra half-hour felt like it went by in two minutes, and off to Great-grandma's bedroom we marched. I thought about my sisters who were probably fast asleep, without a care, in the guest bedroom—the only room we had ever slept in at Nan's house—until right now.

"I'm sleeping in Great-grandma's bed, and Jack is sleeping in the other bed against the wall," I tried to state matter-of-factly to Nan, although I am sure my voice cracked in fear. As soon as Nan left the room, I turned to Jack and whispered, "Remember our deal. You stay awake until I fall asleep, then you can fall asleep." My senses were so heightened, sleep was the last thing on my mind. I could hear the TV. I could smell Great-grandma's perfume.

Eventually, I heard Nan and Pop go to bed. I laid perfectly still as the grandfather clock at the bottom of the stairs chimed eleven times. I was constantly waking Jack up and imploring, "You must stay awake! That was our deal." Sometime before the clock struck midnight, poking Jack on the shoulder to wake him up was no longer successful. I felt so alone . . . or was I.

As midnight approached, I could hear the *tick-tock, tick-tock, tick-tock* of the grandfather clock—the twelve chimes tolling at midnight sent my mind into a tizzy. *Do ghosts only come out after midnight? If so, will Great-grandma be sitting in her yellow-cushioned rocking chair only a few feet from where I laid? Could I even see her? Could she see me? Would she know I was in her bed? What if she wanted to go to bed, as a ghost, and she laid on top of me? Would I die too? Or would her spirit go into me?*

I made one last attempt to wake Jack, but to no avail. I laid on my back with my eyes shut as tight as I could. I didn't want to see Great-grandma in her rocking chair. I didn't want her to come into her bed. I was so scared that tears were flowing down the sides of my face.

I am not certain how long I laid there crying in silence and trembling in fear, but at some point, a hand touched my left shoulder. I opened my eyes and turned toward Jack, "You're awake!" But no, Jack was still fast asleep. Just as I was about to freak out wondering who was touching my shoulder, a warmth started to flow into my body from where this hand was touching me and flowed all the way down to my feet. My body completely relaxed, and my trembling was gone. In fact, it had stopped altogether. Words can never accurately describe the incredible depth of this warmth flowing into my ten-year-old body—a peacefulness and love I had never experienced in my life.

I was not even scared. It was so overwhelmingly peaceful, I didn't even care that something or someone was touching my shoulder—yet my eyes saw nothing through the tears. I felt unconditional love.

Then I heard a voice say my name, "David." It was a deep male voice—not commanding—but full of love. I listened to hear more. "David, your great-grandmother loved you so much. She would never hurt you or scare you." I smiled, wiped away the last of my tears, and whispered "Okay, thank you." And the hand that had been touching my shoulder was gone.

I glanced over at Great-grandma's yellow-cushioned rocking chair. She was not there, but I no longer felt alone. The grandfather clock struck one.

A Spiritual Perspective on Unconditional Love

At the time

The next morning, I awoke with a new perspective on life. I had experienced some type of invisible force filled with love that could talk to me, touch me, take away my fears and my tears. Some type of energetic entity could communicate with us and save us—when we are in distress—without even asking! Was it God? I didn't know. Was it Jesus? I wasn't sure. Was it a guardian angel? I wasn't sure. It didn't matter to me. I started to understand unconditional love from an invisible touch filled with *only love*.

Finding Clarity:

Am I able to feel a loving, peaceful, and joyful personal connection to the Universe?

As I write today

I would truly not physically experience that level of unconditional love from the angelic realm again until my early twenties. It was the first time in my life I was touched by an angel, although it certainly would not be the last. It also would not be for a few more years that I would truly understand the extent of protection afforded to me by the angelic realm. It meant that I was never truly alone in a time of need. It was a source of peace in my soul just knowing there was someone real in an invisible realm who might come to help me when I was scared. That was important to me. I felt safe.

I also learned there are many ways people exhibit love. Even in Great-grandma's stern German way of interacting with us kids, she really did love us. It was just her way. I see that people express love in different ways based upon their upbringing, family history, and personalities. It made me quite aware of how love is expressed, how love is received, and how love can become conditional.

I have also observed that masculine and feminine energies also manifest expressions of love in different ways. We'll have to start way back in human history to decipher this one.

Development of separate genders in humans occurred many millennia ago. I will delve right into the soul energy aspect. In early human development, energy manifested itself differently in the beings who were masculine (as male) versus feminine (as female).

Males, being physically stronger, evolved into the providers for and the protectors of the family/clan/village structure as a survival mechanism. Maslow's hierarchy of needs explains that *physiological needs* are the most basic (breathing, food, water, shelter, clothing, and sleep), followed by *safety and security* (health, property, family protection, and skills). Masculine energy developed to fulfill these needs. In simplified terms, masculine energy traditionally manifests un-conditional love by providing for family needs and protection.

Females, being the bringers-of-life and nurturers, developed their soul energy at a higher level in Maslow's hierarchy—*love and belonging* (friendship, family, intimacy, and sense of connection). In simplified terms, feminine energy manifests unconditional love as human connectivity and nurturing.

Unfortunately, the perception of masculine and feminine energy, as manifested in our time-space physical plane, has been confused. We have created a society where the masculine and the feminine are perceived to be separate—when, in fact, they are not separate at all. Every one of us—*every one of us*—is endowed by the Creator with *both* these energies, the masculine and the feminine. With the ability to exhibit unconditional love within a blend of these energies. No one lacks. We are all whole. And neither is toxic.

At this time in human development, we should all be aware that unconditional love must be extended to those who are struggling with their gender identity—maybe because they are uncertain, or maybe they *are* certain, but not currently accepted by their family.

During our natural progression toward The Golden Age of only-love, humanity will finally become aware that we live in a multi-dimensional existence. Some people may feel disconnected from their own bodies. Some people may feel uncomfortable in their own bodies. Some people may consciously or unconsciously realize that their soul energy exists in other dimensions in a physical body of the *opposite* gender, or *no gender* at all.

Without spiritual awareness, many will have anxiety and may become depressed. Some will commit suicide. Some will change their gender. These are unintended consequences that will spring from the energetic shift presently occurring in our time-space dimension. We should express unconditional love to those experiencing these changes. Luckily, many more people will revel in their growing awareness of self.

For now, simply know that we choose our gender before arriving here in this dimension. It wasn't random. It was for a purpose—maybe to experience the other side of our masculine/feminine energy duality. I wouldn't presume to know what your purpose. I wouldn't presume to know if this is your first time being in a male-gendered body, or vice versa. I wouldn't presume to judge the nature of your physical or sexual attractions. We all have a balance of masculine and feminine energies within us. Unconditional love of this dual energetic nature will lead us to an understanding of a wholeness that has yet to be achieved. Stay true to your natural body. Find the balance of masculine and feminine energies within your soul regardless of your present vessel.

Daily Affirmation

I invite unconditional love into my life,
as both giver and receiver.

"The concept of randomness and coincidence will be obsolete when people can finally define a formulation of patterned interaction between all things within the universe." **~Toba Beta, Betelgeuse Incident**

Chapter Four

Baseball and Guardian Angels

A Spiritual Perspective on Coincidences

I'll Play Baseball in Heaven

David K. Munson ©2020

In *A League of Their Own*,

the *Angels in the Outfield*

are playing on a *Field of Dreams*.

I'm *The Natural* playing in *The Sandlot*,

and I throw my last pitch

in *The Final Season* of life.

Then I rise happily

For Love of the Game.

It was the Spring of 1967. The New York Mets had just started their sixth season. The future was seemingly bright for our Mets, as they had lost only ninety-five games in the 1966 season—an improvement from their first four seasons! I became a Mets fan—in the land of the Yankees—because Nan and Pop just loved to watch the Mets. Every day. Every game. Volume turned up high so they could hear it. We could hear the game too as we played outside in their backyard.

I would hear Nan yell to my Pop many times that season, "What's the score?" Pop would almost always say, "They're losing again!" You see, the New York Mets were a bad baseball team, mostly players at the end of their careers and young kids who wouldn't normally be in the big leagues for other major league baseball teams. Occasionally, I would hear Pop say, "That young kid is pitching good today."

> *[For non-baseball fans, he was referring to a young twenty-two-year-old Tom Seaver, #41, pitching in the rookie season of his hall-of-fame career. He would go on to win 1967 Rookie of the Year. And a few baseball seasons later, he would win the National League Cy Young Award on the team forever known as the Miracle Mets—a story for another time.]*

It's hard to believe it was more than fifty years ago, especially since that was the first time I almost died. I remember that day as if it happened yesterday.

Cousin Jack and I were playing catch in the backyard. Allow me to clarify—baseball. If there was no snow on the ground, we played baseball. You see, when you have a cousin of the same age there is always someone to play catch with—pop-ups, grounders, hitting—you name it, we did it with a bat, a mitt, and a baseball. We even had a pitcher's mound, a pitching rubber, a home plate, and a backstop in my yard. The pitching rubber and home plate were "recovered" from a dumpster after the local little league ballfield at Macghee Park was updated. The backstop was constructed of chicken wire nailed between two pine trees, which were trimmed just high enough to accommodate a wild pitch. No sense breaking a window when you can just nail up more chicken wire on the pine trees!

On this day, Kevin came riding into the yard on his bicycle. "I'm heading for George's Market to get some candy. Wanna come?" he asked. Although Kevin was the starting catcher on our little league team, we usually didn't play together off the field. His other friends must be busy today, I thought. "Sure!" Jack said. I piped in, "I'll go get some money." Just then Kevin said, "You don't need money for candy at George's. You just put it down your pants." I glanced at Jack, and we made fleeting eye contact. "I'll go let my mom know we're going," I stated matter-of-factly, but my real plan was to go in and get my own money to buy my own candy.

Jack and I had made the bike ride through to George's Market many times. I could almost do it with my eyes closed: through my backyard; over the dirt mounds covered with weeds next door—a great opportunity to do wheelies; across the parking lot of the business that sold pre-made concrete steps; cut through the muddy path of cattails; ride across East Bend Road to Macghee Park; along the edge of two baseball fields; across the broken-down asphalt basketball court where there were broken bottles to skillfully maneuver past; into the woods where you would have to get off your bike and strategically step on rocks as you crossed a spring-fed stream; through a farm meadow into the parking lot of the local apartment complex; and finally onto Maloney Road where the last quarter mile was downhill into the George's Market parking lot.

We didn't worry about the mud, streams, weeds, and poison ivy because our one-speed bikes—recycled from someone's garage sale and fixed-up with a little spray paint and new tires—were up for the task! My cousin's second-hand bike was red. I had spray painted my bike a forest green color. I didn't even mind the spots of rust on the handlebars. Jack and I loved our bikes as if they were brand new from Montgomery Ward.

On this day, my ride to George's Market was not so peaceful. I was trying to figure out how to avoid being in the store with Kevin—especially if his plan was to really steal candy. It's hard not being one of the cool kids, but sometimes the price to try is too high. I reviewed my options as I pedaled forward. We could all go in together, and I would quickly pick a Butterfinger bar and get in line to pay so it didn't appear we were together—I was assuming it took time to secretly stuff candy down your pants without anyone noticing. Or, we all go in together, but I go to the ice cream section—I was certain Kevin wasn't going to put ice cream down his pants. Another option was that I could volunteer to watch the bikes while Jack and Kevin go into the store. Unfortunately, this was the worst plan of all options because—in our little neck of the world in 1967—there was no reason to watch your bikes while in the store. We didn't even own bike locks! Or I could just turn around now and go home. Once again, peer pressure to be a cool kid. I couldn't think of a good excuse to turn around. I obviously had a good reason to turn around—but not a good excuse.

Eventually, I settled on the first option—*be quick*—and was relieved when it worked. As Kevin and Jack were leaving George's Market, I was already done with my Butterfinger candy bar ready to ride off—half expecting the manager to be running out of the store to catch Kevin. I hardly waited for them to get onto their bikes and implored, "Let's go now. There's a storm brewing." And how convenient, I thought! So, we quickly left the parking lot, pedaled up the Maloney Road hill toward home in the reverse order we arrived—just as the thunder and lightning started in the distance.

It is difficult to encourage ten-year-old boys to pedal faster when they have chocolate in their hands, but the wind was kicking up. You know—the kind of wind that causes the maple leaves to flip over.

The kind of wind that brings in dark gray storm clouds and horizontal rain faster than you expect. As we approached the spring-fed stream in the woods, we didn't bother to get off our bikes. We rode right through the water as it sprayed up onto our legs, and each other. We didn't care. It seemed like we were going to get wet anyway.

As we approached the Macghee Park baseball fields, where we played our weekly Little League games, the lightning and rain started. I strongly suggested, "Let's duck into the dugout; we are not going to make it home!" We all agreed on that plan, as we ditched our bikes in the dirt and jumped down into the third-base dugout without even touching the two concrete steps. All three of us huddled on top of the players bench with our heads touching the sturdy roof of the dugout—safe from the pouring rain, horizontal wind, black clouds, thunder, and lightning. Safe at last, or so we thought.

I drifted into memories of baseball games played on this ballfield:

> *I love baseball. Three outs. Three strikes. Three bases. Nine innings. Nine players. Ninety feet. Every pitch—a hundred different scenarios with no time limit. The difference between success or failure measured in inches. Images of past baseball games flooded into my head like the water that was flowing down the concrete steps into our dugout shelter. Memories when time stood still, when it was just me on the pitching mound rotating the ball nervously in my hand. Just throw one more strike. Even if he hits the ball, I have teammates backing me up. Wipe the*

sweat off my forehead onto my sleeve. Take a deep breath. The runner on first will be going on the pitch. This moment rests with me—until the ball reaches the plate. The result will no longer be in my control. Will the batter swing? Will the catcher catch the pitch? I hope the ball is hit to Jack at shortstop or to me for the final out. Strike three! Game.

A quick glance toward the first base dugout for a smile from the coach—my dad. It's only brief because I know he will be walking over to the other team's coach to shake his hand and say, "Good game." We were expected to do that after every game—win or lose—no exceptions. It was about respecting the game. It was about respecting the effort of your opponent. It was about not being a sore loser nor a sore winner.

I always glanced into the stands to smile at my mom, Nan, and Pop, who always came to our Little League games—even if the Mets were on TV. After our traditional handshakes and the "2, 4, 6, 8, who do we appreciate . . ." chant, I would walk over to see Nan and Pop. I wanted them to always know I appreciated them coming out to our games. They were not young. The gray-painted wooden bleachers at Macghee Park were not comfortable. When I was in a jam on the field, I always looked for Nan and Pop sitting in the bleachers—they loved me unconditionally. They were happy just to be watching their grandsons play baseball whether we won or lost. It would comfort me and reduce the stress of the moment. After the game, Pop would always recount a play Jack, or I had done during the game. "Your hit in the second inning was a doozy," he would say. Or "Nice pitching, boy. The Mets could use you!"

My daydreams of baseball were suddenly interrupted as I heard my cousin say, "David." I turned to him and asked what he wanted. His reply confused me as he stated, "I didn't say anything." He seemed annoyed. Maybe I was interrupting his own memories of our baseball games played on this very baseball field. I turned back to see the rain was still heavy, and the wind was blowing it side-ways. I was so glad to be in this dugout—safe and dry.

Once again, I heard my name called, but it was a female voice. I heard it clearly over the pounding of the rain on the dugout roof. I turned my head away from my cousin and replied out loud, "What?" The female voice stated firmly, "David. You must leave now!" As I looked out at the storm, I thought of a response so I would be certain of her message, "Do you mean we should leave this dugout and go out into this storm?"

"Yes! You must leave now," came her urgent reply. Okay, if she thinks it is more dangerous to stay in this dugout than to venture into thunder, lightning, and rain, then I must listen to her. It wasn't the first time I heard a voice out of thin air, just like that night in Great-grandma's bed.

I jumped off the bench into the water that was accumulating on the floor of the dugout, turned toward Jack and Kevin, and stated, "We have to leave NOW." They looked at me like I was crazy. Do you blame them? There was thunder, lightning, and horizontal rain just feet from where we were comfortably hanging out in the third-base dugout. And they could see that my sneakers were now soaking wet. They declined my appeal, even after reiterating it for a second time. They weren't budging. I turned and took the two concrete steps up and out of the recessed dugout—right into the storm—where our bikes had been laying in the red mud. I lifted my forest green bike with the rusty handlebars and got on the seat.

Right away, I was soaked through my clothes. As I sat on my bike, I made one last appeal to Jack and Kevin to leave the dugout. "C'mon guys. We must go now. It's not so bad out here," I lied. Once again, they looked at me like I was crazy and said, in unison, "No way!" Frustrated, I said "Fine! I'm going now." They just waved. The memory of that delicious Butterfinger was long gone.

I was so frustrated they wouldn't listen, but I couldn't tell them that I heard a warning. I pedaled my bike around the dugout toward the chain-linked fence, where the gate led to Macghee Road, and on my way toward the warmth of home. As I approached the gate, I saw it was closed and was upset I had to stop and open it. At least I didn't have to get off my bike, I thought. Once opened, I put my foot back on the pedal, pushed hard to get a good start in the mud, and started through that gate opening. Suddenly, as I was half-way through the gate, something pressed across my chest and immediately halted my progress—even though I was still firmly pressing down on the bike pedals. I increased my efforts to get through the gate, but the invisible pressure on my chest increased in proportion to my efforts.

Once again, I heard her voice. "David. Stop! David. Stop!" I put my foot on the ground to steady the bike. The pressure across my chest vanished. Her voice continued, "Go back and get them." I wanted to make sure she heard me over the rain, thunder, and lightning of the storm, so I turned my head skyward and replied loudly, "Go back and get them?" She reiterated calmly, "Yes, David. Go back and get them." My plea to her was desperate, "But they won't come! I need help!"

You see, I now knew this was important to do, but I felt powerless to convince Jack and Kevin to leave, since they were both more stubborn and macho than me. Just then, all I heard in my head were chickens—chickens clucking. Within a few seconds I knew exactly what this message meant. I turned my bike around and rode through the red mud back to the front of the dugout. Jack and Kevin were surprised to see me. They thought I was long gone.

"You guys are so chicken of a little rain," I said with almost a double-dog-dare tone of voice. I followed with the best chicken impression of my life—*cluck, cluck, cluck*. I could see they were getting uncomfortable, as I continued to challenge their manhood. I was hoping they wouldn't beat the snot out of me if I was successful in getting them to leave the dugout and venture out into this storm. I doubled down, "I didn't know you guys were scaredy-cats of a little thunder and lightning."

"No, we're not!" they emphatically replied. *I knew I had them.* "Then prove it," I said in my most firm voice. They huffed and jumped off the dugout bench, into the water at their feet and up the two concrete dugout steps into the storm. After they grabbed their bikes, I let them ride in front of me through the baseball field gate. That was my only way of ensuring I would be able to ride through those gates—*this time.* As I left through the gates, I heard her say, "Thank you, David."

It was only about thirty minutes later that the storm had passed through. During that time, my cousin and I had sat on the back porch without speaking a word to each other. He was watching the puddles in the yard grow larger and branches falling from the pine trees. I was quiet because—to Kevin and Jack—they had gotten soaked in the storm for no apparent reason. The rain was already over. We could have just stayed in that dugout for a short period of time. Really, I was deep in thought about what had just occurred at the ball field. Had I imagined the female voice? Had I imagined what she was saying to me? Why was it a female voice and not the male voice I had heard in Great-grandma's bed? What invisible force had stopped me from pedaling through the gate? That was not my imagination!

It is always an eerie sight to have the sun come out while the remnants of the dark gray clouds, thunder, and lightning can still be seen and heard in the distance—a typical fast-moving spring storm in upstate New York. I wanted to go back to the ball field and get some answers—but I was hesitant to go alone. "Let's go see how wet the ball field is after the storm. We do have a Little League game later this week, I stated in my most responsible voice. Jack agreed, although I could tell he just wanted to go and change into some dry clothes. As we rode back to the ball field, we diverted our trip to enjoy riding through some big puddles—the bigger the splash, the better! Besides, I did not want to seem *too* anxious to get back to the ball field—riding through puddles was normal for us.

As we approached the ball field, my cousin yelled back, "The dugout blew away!" As I looked ahead, I could see the third-base dugout was gone! Wow. I guess it was good we left and weren't in it. As we rode right up to where the dugout had been, it was clear that our first observations were not correct—the dugout had collapsed! The heavy cinder block walls, the shingled roof held up by thick wooden beams had all collapsed onto itself into one big pile of rubble. All you could see were the two concrete steps going down into what was—just less than an hour ago—our shelter from the storm. "Oh my God. We were lucky," Jack exclaimed. I simply replied, "Yup."

David K. Munson

A Spiritualist Perspective on Coincidences

At the time

I think my simple answer "*Yup*" to my cousin was not to be flippant. My reaction was truly reflective of the shock I felt over what had just occurred in the past hour. Sure, I knew there was an invisible force that had come to my assistance in the past, but this was different. I heard a female voice, and she saved my life. Not only that—she saved Jack and Kevin's lives, too. The truth is—it scared me. Not because I came so close to death, but I came so close to letting my ego get the best of me and leaving Jack and Kevin there to die in that third-base dugout. At twelve-years-old, I felt a great responsibility to be aware of my guardian angels' voices—to never ignore them—and protect those who I was with.

As I write today

In this physical world of three-dimensional space, we rely on our physical senses to inform us of the world around us. This thought process creates a sense of "seeing is believing." In fact, some people utilize this premise to conveniently deny the existence of angels, spirit guides, life after death, and even God. They are temporarily anchored to their own disbelief system, not allowing for the possibility my experience in the third-base dugout could have ever occurred. It must have been a coincidence, they might say. They may even ask why it never happened to them in their life, to which

I respond: In disbelief, we create our own self-fulfilling prophecies—what is not acknowledged will remain *un*-seen, *un*-heard, *un*-felt, and *un*-experienced.

It was no coincidence that I heard my guardian angel's warning in the third-base dugout. My belief system was open to that type of communication. Others may have died in that third-base dugout because of ingrained beliefs that would have prevented them from hearing or heeding the dire warnings of their own guardian angels. I pray that everyone is blessed with that level of communication.

Today, Jack has three sons and a daughter with many grand-children and is a youth minister at his church. I'm not sure where Kevin's life took him. But in each moment of time, our impacts are both seen and unseen. We affect each other's journeys. You may understand now why *It's a Wonderful Life* is one of my favorite movies.

As light beings, having a physical experience in this time-space plane, we each have free will to believe or disbelieve at whatever level we so choose. The best thing about free will is you can change your mind. Right now! Right here! I am not asking you to jump into the deep end of the belief pool. All I am suggesting is you remember something in your life that "*was just a coincidence,*" or "*changed the course of your life,*" or when "*you were in the right place at the right time,*" or "*you had a strong feeling to act and it worked out,*" or "*you had a strong feeling to act, didn't act, and it didn't work out,*" or "*a stranger came along to say exactly what you needed to hear*," or "*a book came along with a message just for you.*"

Finding Clarity:
> *Am I able to recognize that I have free will to accept or deny coincidences or serendipitous events as guideposts from a loving Universe?*

I have hundreds of examples throughout my life when I understood that a perceived coincidence was the loving hand of the Universe. I'll just give a simple example of a recent coincidence:

> *My wife and I were invited to Fred and Donna's home for dinner. It was our first time visiting their nice home nestled in the nearby rolling hills. Before dinner, over a glass of wine, the discussion turned to real estate. Fred was lamenting that they had listed a very nice property they owned nearby with a real estate agent who was not very effective or efficient. It had been sitting unsold for more than a year. In that moment, I received a message from my guardian angel. The property needed a For Sale sign because an interested party would soon drive by their property and make an offer to buy it. I was apprehensive to reveal this message because I was unsure of their belief system. So, I just asked, "Does your property have a for sale sign?" Well, for the next*

five minutes Fred went into a tirade about how his real estate agent's sign had fallen down months ago and she was not being responsive to get a new one up. So now I knew the message I received was accurate and decided to deliver it. ". . . so, we have to go now and put the sign back up because someone will be driving by your property soon and make an offer," I stated. "Well, I'm not sure I believe in all that, but putting the sign back up is a good idea. So, let's go do it now," Fred replied. We drove fifteen minutes, put up a homemade for sale sign and returned to our dinner. By dessert, Fred had already received a call from a drive-by interested party. The property was sold within a few days. "Just a coincidence," Fred later recounted.

Coincidence? No such thing. Be thankful for even the smallest of blessings. I also have hundreds of examples where friends, relatives, acquaintances, coworkers, and perfect strangers have confided their stories of coincidences to me—some recalling in belief, some in disbelief, and some telling their story just to receive a sense they were not crazy at the time.

Life presents us with these scenarios every day, as giver and as receiver. In Fred's case, another year-long delay in selling his property was not a life-or-death scenario. In fact, it would have given Fred additional opportunities to complain about the poor service he was receiving from his real estate agent. Once the message was delivered, it was entirely up to Fred to ignore it, think about it, act upon it, or reconfigure it—all viable options he was empowered to choose within a free-will universe.

You are completely free to ignore apparent coincidences or serendipitous events, as if they were not the actual initiating action in a series of events that could have changed your life. Or maybe the pigeon that just pooped on your head as you walked down 5th Avenue was just bad luck and not really an opportunity to pause—just in time to see your old high school sweetheart walking out of the H&M store. Or did it anger you enough to miss the Don't Walk signal, so out into New York City taxi cab traffic you went—tempting fate into another direction. You just must be open-minded. Even just *slight* mindfulness will bring into your life a renewed awareness of coincidences—a belief in co-manifestation with the divine.

Most of us can count on one hand the events on our journey here on Earth that have shaped our lives and the perceived coincidences that accompanied those life-changing events. This slight change in your thought process creates the beginning of your journey where "*believing is seeing.*" And seeing is choosing. And self-aware choosing creates your journey.

Daily Affirmation

I see the divine interaction in what I may have
once believed was just a mere coincidence.

"The vibratory frequency of [love] is infinite . . . it's the interconnection of everything. When I speak of the collective conscious or Universe, I'm referring to Infinite Love to which we're always linked. But when we choose to view life in a limited way, we're disconnecting from this power."

~Dr. Darren R. Weissman,
The Power of Infinite Love & Gratitude

Chapter Five

An Angel, an Ant, and Me

A Spiritual Perspective on Connectedness

Crossing Paths

David K. Munson ©2011

Old man, may I query why you sit on this stump
On the side of this path, near the edge of these woods?
Young lad, here I sit like a log with a bump
Too afraid to move on, judgment looms, as it should.

Old man, may I query why you sit with this fear
On the side of this path, near the edge of these woods?
Young lad, tis a lass whom I held so dear
That I badly treated, didn't love as I could.

Old man, may I query why you sit without love
At the side of this path, at the edge of these woods?
Young lad, I know not how to ask God above
To forgive how I was—don't know that I would.

Old man, tis no coincidence I pass this way
To bring you a message and make your heart sway.
I'm an angel sent by your forgiving spouse
And she saved room for you in the Lord's house.

It was 1971. Carole King, the Carpenters, and the Bee Gees played on my transistor radio that summer. Richard Nixon was our president. The voting age was lowered with the passing of the 26th Amendment. I didn't really care about that. I wouldn't be eighteen for another four years, an eternity to a teenager.

I didn't know it yet, but this was the last summer my family would be camping together at Wilcox Memorial Park in Red Hook, New York, in the lower Catskill Mountains. There were many life-changing events in my future, but all I could think about this summer was the possibility of my first kiss.

But first, let me tell you about camping. The second weekend of every summer we would pack up, load the Coleman tent camper, and literally move our lives to Campsite #24, our small haven within Wilcox Park. Camping was about being with family and friends. It was not only my mom, my dad, and sisters, but also uncles, aunts, and lots of cousins were all there camping for weeks throughout each summer.

In preparation for our summer away from home, Mom would gather the family items on the dining room table. Dad would make sure the Coleman tent camper was ready to roll—tires filled, propane tanks ready, zippers work, ax sharpened, and all the winter dirt hosed off the camper. As we got older, each of us was responsible for gathering our own stuff in preparation for the summer—baseball gloves, Frisbees, Yatzee, playing cards, sleeping bags, cots, pillows, rain gear, swimsuits, fishing poles, fishing lures, coloring books, sunglasses, the latest Hardy Boys mystery, and a supply of brightly colored rags in preparation for our favorite night-time camping game, Capture the Flag.

The night before we left for campsite #24, it was always hard to sleep because we were so excited about the adventures ahead. When morning arrived, we loaded the car quickly in anticipation of our first day at the campground. After hitching up the Coleman camper, we were on our way. As we entered the park, there was a long drive through the fields and woods to our campsite. We knew every turn. In the fields, we would scan the horizon through the car windows to count the groundhogs poking their heads up wondering who had invaded their early summer privacy. The first trip into the campground each year set the groundhog count baseline for the summer—we counted every time we went into and out of the park—and kept track! On this day, our stomachs had butterflies with excitement, as we were always the first family to set up for the summer. It was a matter of pride.

Our family was a well-oiled machine when it came to setting up our campsite. The boys would help Dad with the camper—back it in, level it, and chock the wheels so it didn't roll off the cliff in the middle of the night. Yes, never forget to chock your wheels.

The girls would help Mom set up the blue and orange dining canopy on a level spot near the camper. Each year our campsite would look nearly the same. I liked the consistency. After lunch on the first day, my sisters, cousin, and I took the challenge of searching the campgrounds for big rocks, which would make up our campfire pit for the whole summer, along with the first inventory of firewood. That was the advantage of being first to set up—we were scavengers! There was always the initial warning from our parents to watch out for the albino skunk, a year-round resident of the park that didn't take kindly to being disturbed.

Campfire pit design—placement and construction—was crucial. Every rock we came across would be evaluated with key engineering questions: Can we use it to build the firepit? How heavy is it? Can two of us carry it all the way back to the campsite? Is it a usable shape and size? Does it have a flat bottom to ensure stability? No one wants to be sitting around a campfire if hot rocks are shifting and rolling toward your feet!

There also were other important things to consider as we built our firepit: having enough room for everyone to sit around on their portable camp stools; making the firepit level so we could cook campfire pies without having to hold the handles; and building it away from the dining tarp and overhanging trees. We appreciated being given such a big responsibility. The payoff was big.

During the first campfire gathering of the year, someone would say, "Great campfire pit, Ken!" And my dad would reply, "The kids built it!" There would be smiles and nods of approval from the adults because they knew there would be many memories of fun times around our campfire.

During our scavenging, if we were very lucky, we would find a pile of unused, aged firewood that had been left over from the summer before—therefore delaying our bigger firewood hunt for fresh wood a few more days. If not, the first big firewood hunt of the summer would begin right away.

I always headed for the pine forest up the hill from our campsite. I loved the pine forest—the smell in the air, the wind whistling through the tall branches, the protection I always felt there. And besides, over the winter there were always a few good trees lying on the ground to be dragged out on the first day. My goal was always to come back with the biggest tree log. Of course, it was our job to saw and chop the wood with the freshly sharpened wood saw, ax, and hatchet. Our mom would always remind us to be careful in her own way, "Remember to be careful cutting wood. The hospital is almost an hour away and you don't want to spend the summer unable to swim!" Her advice was good psychology because that warning made us extra careful.

The chopped wood would have to be organized into campfire-sized pieces—kindling in one pile, another pile for medium-sized starter wood, and really good size logs in the third. You know, the ones that could burn all night as you stared at the fire and enjoyed the crackling of pine sap during the first campfire of the summer.

We were given a lot of responsibility, but we also earned the latitude of our chosen summer activities. After our first dinner at camp, our family ritual was to walk to the beach and take our first swim of the year. The beach was closed. It was after hours and there were no lifeguards on duty. There was just sand, water, Mom, Dad, and us kids—initiating a summer of fun within the six-hundred fourteen acres of our favorite park.

The summer days were long—filled with fishing, swimming, hiking, and just lying on the beach in the summer sun. There is something special about lying on the beach with nowhere to go, nothing that needs to get done, and no schedule. We didn't have access to television, nor did we miss it. Time was nonexistent. To us, the outside world was nonexistent.

Most days, my sisters and cousins were the only ones at the beach, with our moms of course. Usually, we started by lining up in the sand—at a temporary starting line made by one of our feet—and racing toward the water, diving in and swimming out into the middle of the lake. First one to the buoy had bragging rights for the day! Sometimes we would just swim laps in the lake, but usually we were making up some type of game all of us could play together—and we had our own rules.

We played water Frisbee to see how many times we could catch it in a row. We always kept track of the record, which usually required diving across the water to make a one-handed save. Our rule was if you went under water during a dive and catch, you had to keep your arm in the air to show you had caught the Frisbee fair and square. The integrity of the Frisbee record was at stake! A game of water Frisbee easily turned into a no rules "pickle-in-the-middle" game, which would quickly degrade into us flailing our arms and pretending to drown. The goal: to predict how long it would take for our mom or aunt to look up from the latest Jacqueline Susann novel to see if we were alright. When they finally did, we would laugh and go on to the next game.

The final two games I remember were treading water and holding your breath. We would go to the deep part of the lake—where no one could touch the bottom—and tread water. Whoever lasted the longest won, and typically my sister, Karen, held that honor. We would also do the same for the "holding your breath under water" contests. I was pretty good at that. Little did I know, but that specific skill would help save my life the following summer.

There was a concession stand at the beach, and I would occasion-ally spend my allowance on french fries and Creamsicles. Mostly, our mom made lunches at the campsite, and we took turns carrying the cooler down to the beach each day. It was part of our responsibilities. We knew by noon we could enjoy a peanut butter and jelly sandwich, which in the summer sun would create the most delicious, melted delight. It didn't matter about the messiness—we just jumped back into the lake.

On many days, if it wasn't my turn to carry the cooler back to the campsite, I would leave the beach early. It was the time I could just be by myself. I would get into some dry clothes, hang my wet bathing suit on the summer clothesline hung between two trees, and write a note—*went for a hike*. I would place the note on the family's picnic table—held down by a rock in a spot that would ensure my mom would see it when they all arrived back from the beach.

I loved hiking in the woods by myself. Sometimes, I would even stay on the marked trails. I enjoyed finding a field of tall grass, or a bed of pine needles, lying down, and just being. I felt invisible to the world. And I especially enjoyed the sound of the wind as it gracefully moved through the tall grass or white pine branches. Many times, my thoughts turned to the experiences I could not share with anyone else—even my siblings. By this summer, I had already known for six years that my soul was separate from my body. I wondered about the hereafter—Heaven if you will. I felt much closer to God walking in the woods or lying in a field of tall grass than sitting in a church pew. I wondered in the grand scheme of life if that belief was okay.

I would think back to Great-grandma's bed, when an angel touched me, and I felt so much love. I had not experienced that level of love and peacefulness since, although I was happy to know Great-grandma must be okay in Heaven. And I thought about being saved by an angel in the baseball dugout two years earlier. Why was I saved? Why do other people die? Why do they get seriously injured in accidents? To me, it appeared God punished some people and not others. By this time in my life, I was also aware others did not have these answers—and maybe didn't even have these questions either—but it did not stop me from taking my hikes alone, contemplating my life and the universe.

I spent hours thinking about what normal fourteen-year-olds thought about—girls I liked, playing baseball, why some boys in school were bullies just because I hadn't grown into my ears yet, and what classes I would have the next school year. This summer, I was looking forward to our camp friends arriving soon.

Life was magical. We always found our own fun and our own adventures: like swimming across the fishing lake at night on a dare; climbing the loose shale cliffs across from the swimming area; walking the swimming lake dam like a balance beam; sneaking into a creepy, old, abandoned house in the woods at night with just a flashlight; staying in camp and riding out a hurricane. These are adventures you might see in a *Johnny Quest* or *Scooby Doo* episode, and we were blessed to live them in real life. Somehow, I feel if my parents were older and more cautious, we would not have had the latitude to experience these adventures.

Was I scared sometimes? Sure. I always said a prayer of protection before the more dangerous adventures. I asked my guardian angels to protect us and *make sure to tell me* if we were in real danger—you know, just like when my cousin, friend, and I were saved from the collapsing baseball dugout two years earlier. I was always listening to hear *her* voice. I listened before we jumped in to swim across the whole fishing lake at night in the dark. I listened before we started to climb thirty feet up the steep shale cliff adjacent to the park entrance road. I listened for her protective presence during the hurricane, even though my parents had reassured us everything would be okay. I felt protected.

Nighttime was magical at the campground, too. The smell of campfires wafting through the air mingled with muffled conversations and outbursts of laughter. Our favorite nighttime game was Capture the Flag. With more than six hundred acres in the park, we had very specific boundary rules on where the flags could be hidden—roughly a ten-acre area was considered in bounds. Many nights, the beauty of the night sky and the fullness of the stars distracted me. Sometimes I would purposely volunteer to guard the flag in a field, just so I could lay there and watch the sky. So many stars to look at. For me, my guidepost was the constellation Orion. I always felt more grounded when he was guarding the night sky.

Of course, I was always aware to watch out for the albino skunk wandering through the woods near our campground. I was deathly afraid of that skunk for years. I guess we were connected some-how, or I was having premonitions, because it wandered under our camper one night, was startled by our dog Bingo, and sprayed just a few feet from my head. To this day, I still get nauseated when I smell a skunk!

Natalie. That's the girl I thought would be my first kiss. Her family would camp during the special holiday weekends for the past few summers, and Memorial Day was coming up. It would be the first busy camping weekend when the part-timers came to the campground. Most of the rest of the summer, the whole campground was just ours. My sister, Karen, was excited because Alex, Natalie's older brother, was coming to camp this year. I was particularly excited because Natalie would be there, too. She was more my type than my cousin's type. He tended to like giggly blondes, while I was more attracted to studious brunettes. Natalie was the latter, with long, dark hair that shimmered like silk in the summer sun. And she was smart, too! At least that's what I recalled from the summer before . . . when I was only thirteen.

On the day they were scheduled to arrive, we waited in the playground, near where Natalie and Alex's parents usually set up their camp. It was a good look-out spot for us. We didn't want to appear too eager or desperate for friends, but we wanted to appropriately greet them. The playground was a good compromise location. Besides, there is something about a good swing that can calm the nerves and take those pesky butterflies away from the stomach. As their truck and camper pulled into the campground, we waved and continued to swing and seesaw. We knew the drill. Kids first help set up camp—then the fun could begin.

By the next day, it was sadly clear to me I was the fifth wheel. Alex and Karen were already holding hands. Natalie was fully flirting with my cousin, Jack. Even at this age, I had already had enough experiences with girls who were attracted to my blonde-haired blue-eyed cousin. He had freckles, too. It was another reminder that I was the brown-haired nerd with glasses, and I hadn't quite grown into my ears yet. By Saturday evening, Natalie and Jack were holding hands, too, and she had already kissed him! That was supposed to be my kiss. That night, I sat around the campfire with the adults, making an excuse that I didn't exactly feel well. It wasn't too far from the truth.

The next morning, I awoke early as usual. I loved being the first one awake. Quietly, I would dress and slowly unzip the canvas tent so as not to wake the others. On this morning, I was extra quiet, as I wanted to be alone in my sadness. As I walked to the restrooms, I could tell it was still early summer when mornings are still cool, and the dew is heavy on the grass. There was a chill in the air mixed with the smell of early morning campfires and bacon. I returned to our campsite and started a morning fire so the others could be warm when they woke up. Despite my sadness, there was no place in the world I would have rather been.

Since I was relegated to fifth wheel status, and wasn't good company anyway, I decided to spend the day hiking solo. I could choose between my favorite hikes at Wilcox Park: the marked trail through the pine tree forest; the open field hilly hike with the nice view; or hike on an unmarked trail by the stream that ran next to the campground. I chose the unmarked trail.

I love water, especially running water. It calms me. That felt like the best thing for me to do, so off I went blazing my own trail toward a stream that ran through the park. The first portion of the hike wasn't so pleasant, as the stream was surrounded by muddy wetlands filled with wetland cabbage. If you know anything about the outdoors, you know why this large-leafed plant is commonly known as skunk cabbage. Just part of the adventure, I thought, and traveled on for a while despite the temporary odor issue. I was hoping the albino skunk was not hiding among the foliage. At least it kept my mind off matters of the heart.

Up ahead, I spotted a tree that had fallen across the stream where the water was now about six feet wide and a few feet deep moving over rocks on a slight, gentle, downhill slope. This was the perfect spot to stop, rest, and reflect. I scooted across and perched myself in the middle of the log right above the stream. My dangling legs were still a few feet above the water's surface, not that it would have mattered. My Pro Keds sneakers were already wet and muddy from the swampy skunk cabbage portion of my journey. This was a beautiful and peaceful setting. In all the summers at Wilcox Park, I had never been to this spot sitting over the stream in the woods—in the middle of a skunk cabbage patch—where no one else dared to tread.

It had been worth it, I thought, as I reached in my pocket for the Drake's Funny Bone that I brought with me. You know, the peanut-butter-filled chocolate cake with the chocolate coating. Yum! As I ate my Funny Bone, I focused on a group of ants along the edge of the stream. They seemed to be looking for a way to cross the stream as they searched for food. At least they didn't have to worry about their first kiss. I tossed a piece of my Funny Bone in their direction. They were unaware of the yummy chocolate cake lying in the mud just inches from where they were wandering. By the time I swallowed my last morsel of the peanut buttery chocolate snack cake, the sadness had returned to my heart. In fact, my sadness hit my heart so hard I couldn't keep it in. As tears ran down my cheeks, the words streamed from my mouth, "Why God? Why is life so unfair? Why do all the girls like my cousin because he has blonde hair, blue eyes, and freckles?" By the end, my voice became louder as the buildup of my pain was rushing out of my mouth—and right to God's ears.

"It is part of the growing up process. It will not always be this way," was the response I heard. My heart jumped as I turned my head to the left to get a clearer focus on who may have snuck up through the skunk cabbage and heard my lament. As I wiped away my tears, there was no one else in these woods—only the sounds of water rippling over rocks and a few sparrows twittering about in the trees. In a split second, memories came rushing in. I recognized that voice! It was the same deep, gentle, male voice I heard in my great-grandmother's bed four years earlier. Take my word for it, you don't forget that kind of stuff.

All I could muster in the moment was "What did you say?" Not sure why, but I leaned forward trying not to fall off the log into the water below, as if I was expecting the message to be hard to hear. It was clear. I heard his voice again state matter-of-factly, "It is a part of growing up. It will not always be this way." Oh—hmmm—wow. I could now tell the voice was coming from in front of me to the left up toward the sky. I scanned the forest canopy for signs of a person, but no one was there.

Since I had received an answer to my first question, I decided to ask another, "I think I recognize your voice. Are you the one who spoke to me in my Great-grandma Schrauth's bed?"

"*Yes,*" came the reply. So being the curious teenager I was, I decided to continue our conversation.

"How do you know that it will not always be this way, that girls will always like my cousin and not me?"

> "*This is a temporary situation that is part of the growing process. There is a girl already chosen for you that you will meet in the future.*"

"How will I recognize her?"

> "*You will know.*"

"How?"

"*You will just know it is her.*"

"When?"

"*When the time is right.*"

"Okay. I can be patient. I do feel so much better now though. Thank you."

"*You are very welcome.*"

"Can I ask you some other questions that have been on my mind?"

"*Yes.*"

"Can I ask about God?"

"*Yes.*"

"Does God get involved in the details of our lives?"

"*God influences lives, but people can still choose their own way.*"

Wow. That was a very interesting concept to me. I still needed clarification, so I created a scenario about the ant that I had just been observing moments before.

"There is an ant struggling to find a way to cross this stream, yet it has no idea I am up here on this log watching. I could reach down, pick up the ant, carry it across the stream, and place it safely on the other bank. The ant could view that action as a miracle performed by an overseeing loving God or most likely not even be aware that a life-changing event has occurred. Are people like that ant, where the hand of God impacts our lives without our awareness?

"*Yes, that could happen.*"

"Well, I could alternatively choose to just watch the ant struggle or, even worse, I could jump off this log and crush the ant with my foot. The other ants would view this as God's punishment or create a story about how it was well-deserved. Is this how God impacts our lives in a punishing manner?"

"*No. God is only Love.*"

"What? God is only Love?"

"*Yes.*"

"Then where is the punishing God?"

"*There is no punishing God. People already punish themselves and each other enough. God is present to help each person heal.*"

"Oh! Thank you for helping me heal my sorrow."

"*You are welcome.*"

"Can I ask you more questions?"

"*Yes.*"

"Are there other worlds in the universe?"

"*Yes.*"

"How many?"

"*More than you can imagine.*"

"Wow! I always had that feeling. Can I ask you about the nature of the universe?"

"*Yes.*"

"People are made up of atoms with electrons rotating around a central nucleus. That is the same design as our own solar system with planets rotating around the Sun. Is that part of God's design?"

"*Yes.*"

"So, are we living on an electron-like planet rotating around a nucleus-like sun in the body of God?"

"*Similar to that, but so much more complex that it could not be understood by you at this moment in time.*"

"Okay. Thank you for today. Thank you for coming to me in my great-grandma's bed, too. I love you."

"*I love you, too.*"

Somehow, I knew our conversation had ended. I felt at peace. I had no more of the sadness that had led me to this log over this stream in these woods. I looked down to see if I could see the ant. It had moved on. I had moved on. The pain and sadness had been replaced by love and forgiveness. I felt blessed to be connected to a larger Universe.

A Spiritual Perspective on Connectedness

At the time

I continued my solo hike that day with my head spinning, and my heart healed. So much to think about. I am normal. There is a girl already out there for me. God does not punish. And the universe is complex. Phew. Just another day in the life of a fourteen-year-old.

I thought about how I had projected parental qualities onto God. I had the incorrect perception that God doles out punishment, even punishment worse than the belt. I perceived He would not have the time or would not bother to pay attention to a kid. These parental qualities of punishment were certainly reinforced as I attended church services endorsing the concept of living a God-*fearing* life. My heart's desire was to live a God-*loving* life.

During this time, I was still a bit confused about who was communicating with me. I wasn't scared, but when I truly asked from deep down in my soul, that same deep, loving, male voice was there to answer and reassure me. I assumed it was either God directly or his representative. Maybe it was Jesus. Maybe my guardian angel, Nathaniel. When I almost died in the baseball dugout, it was a female voice I heard that saved our lives. My life protector seemed to be a female guardian angel. Cool.

I was no longer angry about Natalie and Jack because I now understood this situation was a normal part of growing up. Knowing that helped so much through high school, as girls continued to flock toward other guys. I was always relegated to the nice guy who was good at listening, as many broken-hearted teenage girls would come to me for a comforting shoulder to cry on, a kind word, and an understanding heart after their boyfriends treated them badly. I was okay with this role, as it helped me develop a very insightful understanding of the female gender—and a very confused view of why guys treated girls so badly. I clearly did not understand typical male human behavior. It impacted my view of relationships—not to take advantage of girls on the rebound, not to start a relationship just because I had the opportunity, and not to go too far sexually in a relationship unless I knew she was the one who had been promised.

Most of the time as a teenager, I tried to do the right thing. I certainly had a different perspective of the Universe and of God's love. And that there was a girl out there for me. I just wasn't sure what the sign would be when she showed up in my life.

As I write today

Through my growth in spiritual understanding, I tell you this simple truth—*God does not punish us.* We move through our space and time existence believing that fear, conditional love, sickness, accidents, control, prejudice, and death are all tools of a punishing, higher authority. God does not exhibit the human parental qualities of punishment. We have projected those qualities onto Him as a convenient excuse for the disconnectedness we created in our world all by ourselves. We have a knack for punishing ourselves, judging ourselves, judging each other, killing each other, isolating each other based upon religion, skin color, race, politics, wealth, and a thousand other dividing concepts that encourage human disconnectedness.

Human disconnectedness also keeps us from acknowledging another simple truth—*we are all energetically connected to each other in God's Universe*. Simply said, what we do to others, we do to ourselves. In the proverbial sense—what goes around, comes around. Or in the biblical sense—for whatever a man sows, that he shall also reap.

People who are made to feel outcast—by society, by social media, by peers, by coworkers, by religion, by government—have the potential to act out in negative ways against themselves and/or others. People who feel disconnected—from God, from love, from family, from society, from forgiveness, from closeness—may act out to harm others or themselves, emotionally and/or physically. These situations negatively impact mental health. And those with mental health struggles may have less capacity to grow their *spiritual wealth*.

Unfortunately, creating disconnectedness is much more prevalent in our society today. We must understand what disconnected looks like, feels like—so we can reverse it and become connected once again. So, let's start there.

Recognizing Spiritual Disconnectedness

Technology, smart phones, social media, Candy Crush—all marketed to connect the world—are the main weapons for our *disconnection* from each other. Even a pandemic with a survival rate greater than 98% for most of humanity, was used to disconnect us from each other. True human connectedness is the enemy of those dark forces moving in to control humanity as prisoners of technology.

And in today's world, they can't allow those prisoners to wake up. The darkness cannot allow those who are asleep staring at their cell phones to awaken. So, the darkness starts one of their clever marketing schemes . . . give up your freedom for the safety of all. Give up your voice so as not to offend someone. Clever marketing. Creating prisoners. The clever, but dark, marketing machine has even taken it to another extreme where they have convinced many people to blame the *tools of violence* instead of recognizing the disconnected soul of the perpetrator. Was that soul taught from an early age, and even conditioned, to act destructively against others without the benefit of creating an account filled with spiritual wealth?

Should we blame the dogwood tree for Jesus' crucifixion? Should we blame the barbed wire fence for the Holocaust? Should we blame the cotton plant for slavery? Should we blame the smallpox-infected blankets for the destruction of the Native American legacy? Should we blame the gun, not the disconnected soul pulling the trigger?

Should we blame violent video games for a generation of disconnected youth and gang violence? Well, maybe. Although, in the end, there is a brainwashed, damaged, numb, incorrectly-medicated, and/or disconnected soul that escalates it from a violent video game and implements it into our reality. In a posting dated March 18, 2017 on *thegamer.com*, their article, *The 15 Most Despicable Acts Committed in Grand Theft Auto*, states:

> "Of course, beating people with baseball bats, shooting them with small arms and driving full speed into them with vehicles is one thing, but part of the **beauty** [emphasis added] of this series is that they've sold over 250 million games by allowing the player to get more creative than that."

This same website's article gave accolades to these violent actions that were added to the newest game version of Grand Theft Auto, including drowning people, targeting cops, reenacting 9/11, blowing someone up on national TV, and torture. Especially revolting is their statement about Killing Ladies of the Night to get your Money Back, where they state:

> "The fact that one can then kill that lady of the night and retrieve that money is just economically sound financial planning."

In what world is any of that okay that we let our teenagers (or younger) participate in such hate and violence—and call it a game? It is simply a *tool* marketed to an unaware population.

On a small scale, every weekend in the streets of Chicago, or on a larger scale in wars around the world, disconnected souls make decisions to escalate violence. Yet, the ones who control the prevailing marketing narrative continue to blame the tools of violence. Why? Because they want you to personally relinquish your protection, your safety, your peace of mind, your voice, your time, your gender, your family, your common sense, your God, and your soul—to them. That's when we will have lost the spiritual war for humanity. Without a moral reset in our society, a continued escalation of man's inhumanity to man will be our society's legacy. No matter what tools are used.

On a more uplifting note, we can reverse this trend. And this is how:

Rebuilding connectedness starts with the family structure. According to the Institute for Family Studies, only 9% of children were raised without their father in 1960, yet today 25% of American kids are raised without a father in their lives. The National Fatherhood Initiative estimates more than 18.4 million children are fatherless.

According to the website *fatherhood.org*, these children are more likely to commit crime, carry illegal guns, go to prison, use drugs and alcohol, and exhibit behavioral problems, just to list a few of the negative outcomes. Kudos to those who have overcome that initial deficit in their lives. It was no small task. The following explanation is from *ifstudies.org*:

One contributor to family breakdown, which soon spread to the poor and working-class white family, may have been welfare expansion. [...] Under [Democrat President] Johnson's Great Society, which began in 1964, benefits became substantially more generous and came under greater control of the federal government.

In the words of Harvard's Paul Peterson, "some programs actively discouraged marriage," because "welfare assistance went to mothers so long as no male was boarding in the household. Marriage to an employed male, even one earning the minimum wage, placed at risk a mother's economic well-being." Welfare workers would randomly appear in homes to check and see if the mother was accurately reporting her family status.

The benefits available [to fatherless homes] were extremely generous. That may be a reason why, in 1964, only 7% of American children were born out of wedlock, compared to 40% today. As Jason Riley has noted, "the government paid mothers to keep fathers out of the home—and paid them well."

Our government funded the disconnection and destruction of the family structure, especially devastating to the stability of families of color. They easily justified the government expense, as a method of dismantling and destabilizing families. It's no wonder that youth gangs, along with their violence, have replaced a fatherless family structure. Our present government could easily reverse this trend through updated laws and redirected funding to encourage family stability. Our voices must be louder. Our prayers must be stronger.

Fund school choice. Stability and morality must continue in the classrooms of our children's schools. If your child is learning that the color of their skin or their gender makes them a victim or an oppressor, rather than how to read, then get them out of there! When I was a teacher, we focused on twenty-first century critical thinking skills, not how to blindly follow compliance dictates. Be very suspicious of anyone who is against school choice.

Wouldn't it be a wonderful world if our children learned the basics of spiritual wealth—love, gratitude, grace, and prayer—alongside the basics of math, science, reading, and the arts? If this describes your child's school, count your blessings.

Protect the constitution. Your enemies are those people who want to disconnect you from your right to free speech, disconnect you from your right to worship, and disconnect you from your right to protect yourself. Those who think the United States Constitution is a living, malleable, changeable document don't accept that it was a God-inspired document. Their strategy is to destroy that document in today's spiritual war. It might even be the central strategy to defeat souls who are empowered by God. One side in this earthly conflict will be looking for your voluntary compliance—*during the next pandemic or climate heat wave crisis*—when you are not allowed to gather, not allowed to worship, not allowed to write this book.

You may not agree with everything I have written, but I'm sure we can agree that you have a God-given right to read it and decide for yourself!

But what if the forces implementing spiritual disconnectedness were ready and waiting at your doorstep to enforce blind obedience to their false god of control. The United States Constitution is the linchpin that holds together our freedom to worship God, in whatever manner we so choose.

Recognizing Spiritual Connectedness

Now, let's take a deep dive, so to speak, into the scientific pool to discuss the electromagnetic energy that flows through our universe and connects us all. This universal energy of our Oneness exists within the electromagnetic spectrum because we are "beings of light." As Pam Grout points out in her New York Times best seller, *E Squared*, "We're all connected to this huge data bank, and we constantly exchange energy with everyone in our circle of influence, and in smaller ways, with every other being on the planet." This is the basis for our connection to the Oneness of God, and to each other.

This concept of electromagnetic energy connection—*corded energy* to each other and to a greater Universe—may seem weird. Just think if you tried to explain a cell phone to Leonardo Da Vinci six-hundred years ago—a man-made technology that connects our conversations through the air. Wait, he probably would have understood that, so we'll go with Ptolemy, the astronomer who believed the Sun orbited around the Earth. After your explanation of cell phone technology, he probably would have thought you had lost your mind. Even a few hundred years ago, humanity would call your explanation of a cell phone either crazy, looney, or maybe even part of a conspiracy theory! Or in Salem, Massachusetts, you may have been burned at the stake by a mob of righteous citizens.

It may be difficult for us to imagine that we exist in an ocean of electromagnetic frequencies we can't see, touch, feel, or smell. All life on planet Earth has evolved in—and exists in—a sea of the electromagnetic spectrum, both natural and man-made.

Mostly, we only *observe* the effects of electromagnetic energy. For example, we see sunlight appear in the morning, even though we can't touch, hear, or smell the eight-minute, thirty-second journey that ray of sunshine took to reach Earth. We feel the warmth of the energy contained within the sun's emissions as it reaches our skin.

Does it require faith in the unseen to successfully use a microwave oven? At some point, we observe the effects, and our Marie Callender's microwavable chicken pot pie is ready to eat! We conclude that electromagnetic frequencies must exist—and they surround and connect us—just like the air we breathe. Whether we realize it or not, we live in a matrix of electromagnetic frequencies.

This concept may seem very otherworldly—so I'll share my fish metaphor:

> *There were three fish in a lake just hanging out when a worm fell into the water near them. How lucky they thought! The first fish said, "There's no such thing as a free lunch—there's always a catch!" The second fish said, "I know some fish would think this is a sign from Heaven, but I don't believe there is any other existence except this beautiful world we live in." The third fish said, "Well, I don't understand what either of you two are carping about, but I'm hungry." And the third fish gulped down the worm and suddenly was gone—pulled out of their lake world. The other two fish thought, "Our friend is gone forever."*
>
> *Well, what happened next may be a fish tale too incredible for my readers to believe! That third fish reappeared minutes later with an incredible tale—a fish tale so to speak. He started in on his story, "As I was being pulled upward, there was a bright light. It was hard to breathe. I thought I was fried. But two huge entities, crowned with baseball caps, grabbed me, smiled at each other, and tossed me back toward our lake world. More incredibly, I saw a sign—a divine message—that read, "All fish in this lake are catch and release. Please throw them back into the water."*
>
> *After listening to his friend's experience, the first fish said, "I'm a skeptic, and I don't really believe there is an existence after we*

leave the lake world. Did you bring back proof?" The third fish replied sheepishly, *"No."* There was a long pause in the conversation. The awkward silence was finally broken when the second fish asked, *"I know we identify as fish, but what is water?"*

Of course, the water keeps them safe, carries life-sustaining nutrients and oxygen, along with providing a mechanism for them to interact physically with the rest of their underwater world. What the fish can't differentiate is that their world of H_2O exists within another realm—called Earth! Their capacity to understand is limited to their senses.

You may consider this unnatural or unbelievable but allow me to use few examples of the amazing ways animals on our planet have naturally evolved while living in this sea of electromagnetic energy. They have most definitely acquired well-developed senses beyond our own present human capabilities:

- The domestic cat and humans can hear the same low frequency (low pitch) sound waves, but cats are born with the ability to hear high frequency (high pitch) sounds in our world, more than quadruple the high-pitched frequencies humans can hear. Just because we can't hear it doesn't mean it doesn't exist or that other species can't hear it. Our ability to hear is constrained to a very narrow spectrum of sound wave frequencies.

- African bush elephants are recognized as having the best sense of smell in the animal kingdom, even greater than a black bear that can smell food more than ten miles away. Just because we can't smell it doesn't mean it doesn't exist, or that other species can't smell it, too. Our ability to smell is constrained by the number of olfactory nerves in our noses. The world must be a very smelly place to elephants and bears.

- Bumblebees have developed an amazing ability to search out which flowers have the most pollen. They detect the flower's *electric field aura,* which changes as the flower blooms and generates pollen. Just because we can't see it doesn't mean the electric field doesn't exist, or that other species can't find it. Our ability to visualize electric fields (auras) surrounding living things is constrained to a narrow group of highly aware humans.

- Humpback whales navigate through the ocean using an ability to detect, analyze, and remember the differences in Earth's electromagnetic field. That ability allows them to annually travel long distances and end up in the same exact location—a natural geographical positioning ability. Our natural ability to derive a sense of direction varies greatly. Unfortunately, their ability to properly navigate has been impacted by undersea internet and windfarm cables giving off man-made electromagnetic signals. Many whales have accidently beached themselves on the east coast and died. Incredibly, the media continues to blame Covid for these tragedies, so as to not offend the wind farm proponents.

As humans, we are familiar with much of the electromagnetic spectrum in our daily lives. To name a few instances that you will easily recognize: the visible light spectrum (the rainbow of colors ROYGBIV); microwaves (that invisible energy that heats our Lean Cuisine); ultraviolet (from the sun that causes our skin to burn); AM/FM/Sirius radio waves (from country stations to classic rock); x-rays (oh, that last dentist root canal); infrared (that thermal imager used to see heat signatures in the dark); and 5G (cell phone towers). These are just some of the electromagnetic frequencies that have been harnessed to help mankind in our physical world—only during the past two-hundred years of human ingenuity.

Connectedness is one of the greatest challenges of our time. Our natural electromagnetic frequencies that connect us with each other, and with the greater Universe, have been contaminated by technology. Contaminated with all the thousands of man-made devices creating unnatural electromagnetic frequencies streaming through our present time-space existence. All this man-made technology interferes with our natural abilities, as beings of light, to feel connected to our natural energy cords, to the Universal energies, and to each other.

It is no wonder that more and more people in our physical time-space existence feel disconnected. It's no wonder the suicide rate is so high—souls just want to reconnect with the hereafter because they feel lost and alone here. It's no wonder that disconnected souls create chaos and violence. But how does one re-connect? How does one reach out? How does one heal?

My simple advice—and my own greatest personal challenge—is to find quiet space, begin to disconnect from man-made technology, and reconnect with our natural abilities. Each one of us is connected to the Oneness of Universal energy and directly *energy-corded* to others within our circle.

Some people connect through quiet meditation, some through introspective reading. Me? I find it when my hands are entrenched in the garden touching the earth or feeling the energy of this planet coursing through an old forest tree or immersing myself in the energy generated by the movement of water flowing along a mountain stream. By grounding to the Earth, we calm the nervous system—the electrical connections in our body. Just like driving a copper stake into the ground to electrically protect buildings, we need a mechanism to rid our bodies of excess nervous impulses created by stress or impacts from unnatural electromagnetic inputs. As an example, my arms tingle when driving under high tension electrical wires. All we have to do is put our hands in the Earth, wrap our arms around a tree, or simply walk through the grass or a sandy beach in bare feet. That's what I mean by *grounding* oneself.

Finding Clarity:

> *Am I able to feel my own personal connection to the vast Oneness of the Universe, to God, to guardian angels, and to other human souls?*

Our natural abilities, which we have denied for so long, enable us to communicate with each other across physical distances. And with our loved ones across the veil. And with our guardian angels. And with God. It is your free-will choice to reach out or not. One of my favorite spiritual songs is *Turn Your Radio On,* written by Albert Brumley, Sr.—a metaphor for opening your heart and mind to the vibrational frequency of the Universe. And to see, hear, and feel God's existence and messages of love.

Allow yourself the space to be present in the blessings of this life—to open your heart, your eyes, and your ears to the feelings, sights, and sounds of an existence that extends beyond our five limited senses. Be open. Be present. Be grateful.

There is peace in knowing every one of us is connected to the energy of Oneness. Simply see others in the light of love. I know that can be hard. Practice forgiveness by sending out a prayer of healing. Minimize judgment by blessing others on their individual journey—because it's *their* journey. By doing this, you have increased your own spiritual wealth.

At the highest level of universal energy—where space and time do not exist in a physical plane—we are all connected. That's where we started, and that's where we are going back to—when our Earth-bound journeys are done.

Daily Affirmation

Thank you for empowering me to quiet my mind,
open my heart, and bring me awareness of
my connectedness to the Universe.

"Birth, life, and death are transitions. Such transitions are not predestined; rather, spirit and body progress in accordance with a blueprint that can be altered by our choices."

> ~**Bryan Christopher,** ***Being Light:***
> ***A Guide to Living in Multidimensional Realities***

Chapter Six

Our Creek

A Spiritual Perspective on Choice

Rachel's Ripple in Time

David K. Munson ©2021

Across time and space,
a person creates a ripple.
A shift in the course of humanity.
Impacting choices to be born upon this Earth,
impacting decisions on when to leave.

Unknown to many that Rachel said,
"But man is a part of nature,
And his war against nature
is inevitably a war against himself."

I propose this ripple—
But man is a part of the One,
and his war against Oneness
is inevitably a war against himself.

I love water. Well, allow me to clarify. I love to be *near* water. I love the feel of water, and I love how it makes me feel. I feel peace sitting by a calm lake. I feel the flow of energy when I am near a moving stream. I enjoy rain. I am calmed by snow. I love the serenity of a foggy morning. I love water in all its forms. It was not always this way for me.

It was the summer of 1961. "Change into your bathing suits. We are going swimming," my mom announced. I asked her where we were going. "We are going across the street to meet our neighbors and swim with them. They have two boys who are a little older than you and the boys are twins," my mom said with a nervous determination in her voice. Looking back, it is understandable she was nervous. She was only twenty-four years old. She was sending me to kindergarten before I turned five, and she wanted me to meet other kids in the neighborhood. I remember not wanting to go. I hated baths, and why would I want to swim in someone else's pool? Besides, I already had best friends—my younger sisters, Karen, and Sue and my cousin Jack. We were all nearly the same age.

"Look both ways," my mom cautioned before we crossed our busy country road. She really didn't need to warn me as we had already lost two cats on New Hackensack Road. Poor Puff. Poor Buff. We crossed the road safely and started downhill on a long driveway.

I can still hear my mom saying, "Don't drag your life preserver." As the driveway curved to the right, I saw the white, cottage-style house where we were heading. I looked around for the pool but was distracted by Mrs. Schroeder stepping out of her house to greet us. Trailing behind were two boys, each with a hand gripping onto their mother's sundress. I grabbed my mom's leg. As we hid behind our moms, introductions proceeded. Paul and Mike were a year older than me and they were going into first grade already. Mike was the twin with the dark hair, like me. Paul was the twin with the light hair. "I am glad you could join us for a swim," Mrs. Schroeder greeted us. She turned to her boys and said, "Take your new friend down and show him the creek, but don't go in until we get there!" *Wait a minute. Where's the swimming pool? Are we swimming in a creek?*

As my mom was strapping on my orange life preserve, I watched Paul and Mike run down the eight wooden steps to the water's edge and jump right in. They didn't even need life preservers. I sat on the bank watching my new friends splash around. We were at an inlet where the creek was wide and slow moving, but I did see rapids—fast moving water with whitecaps—that started about a hundred feet downstream. That was too close. What if I started floating downstream with my life preserver? Could my mom save me?

I heard my mom telling the story about swimming in this creek when she was younger, downstream at Rymph's Farm, I think she said. She described a rope swing hanging from a big tree and the fun times with high school friends. I couldn't imagine her doing that. "Well then," Mrs. Schroeder offered, "why don't you go in for a dip?" After a few minutes, I could see my mom could really swim, and she could probably save me if I drifted toward the rapids or slipped out of my life preserver. I started into the water hoping a fish would not touch my leg. I survived my first experience with the creek. I would come to love Wappinger Creek. I would come to love Paul and Mike.

Paul, Mike, Jack, and I grew up in this stretch of Wappinger Creek. It was *our* creek—the half-mile stretch from the Red Oaks Mill falls to the rapids that began just past their house. I always loved walking to Red Oaks Mill so I could stop on the bridge and watch the falls. To me, it was as if Wappinger Creek began there, instead of where it really began, in Thompson Pond, many miles north.

The creek was calm and deep just before the falls, as it flowed past the Warnock House Restaurant where my parents were married. Pop even had a photograph of the falls hanging in his den. Even in my grandfather's younger years, the falls appeared majestic. There is something beautiful about calm water falling to another level into a turmoil of white-capped rapids. I would watch for hours as

the rapids disappeared under the Red Oaks Mill bridge. The sound was awesome. The movement of water was energizing to me. In all those years, I never went down to the banks of the creek near the falls. I had recurring nightmares about falling in the creek, going over the falls, and barely surviving the rough rapids under the bridge.

Downstream from the falls, the creek widened and became calm. We spent many hours together fishing from the banks of our creek. We would pack a lunch and fish 'til the sun was setting, or 'til we caught enough to eat, or 'til we got hungry, or 'til we ran out of crawfish bait, or 'til we got in a fight with each other.

The best fishing spot was Schofield's dock where the creek was deepest—way over our heads. The sun would warm up the concrete dock nicely on a cool summer day, and I felt safe. One of us would always keep an eye out for Ol' Man Schofield, who didn't want us fishing from his dock. We would catch sunnies, crappies, small-mouth bass, perch, and catfish. We always made sure to leave no mess behind. And we could always count on my mom to clean and cook the big fish we brought home.

Quite frankly, I do not even have one memory of a specific conversation with my cousin or best friends while fishing. We just enjoyed being together. I do recall some lessons that may be applied to any part of life: always respect nature; it's okay to relax and watch the current flow past; don't take more from the earth than you will need that day; always throw back a small fish or a fish that is full of eggs; it's okay to wonder what's upstream; and don't leave behind a mess because it travels downstream. Most importantly, I think we were living in the moment. Four boys. One creek.

A few winters of my childhood, Wappinger Creek froze solid. Solid enough for us to ice skate on it, at least up to the rapids just past Paul and Mike's house. It was like our own private skating area. Paul, Mike, Jack, and I would play hockey for hours. We had our own house rules—no hard checking with the hockey sticks because if they broke, our parents may not be able to afford to buy us another.

The most important rule was no hard puck passes in the direction of the rapids. You know about hockey pucks—they just keep on sliding. If we were lucky, the puck would stop before it fell into the open waters of the rapids where no ice dared to tread. Whoever hit the puck there would have to be tied with clothesline rope, crawl on their belly toward the rapids as the ice made cracking sounds and reach as far as they could with their hockey stick to get the puck back. At times, the four of us would just helplessly watch as our only puck slid toward the rapids where the ice ended. Plop. Into the rapids. Our only puck. We would quickly take up a collection of coins and convince one of our parents to drive us to Montgomery Ward for a new one. You never knew how long the ice would last. And there was more hockey to play.

By the summer of 1972, I had lost touch with our creek. I had spent the prior four summers camping with my family away from Red Oaks Mill. But now, I was home for the summer. My parents had divorced. Things had changed.

When I wanted to be alone, I would take a walk to visit the old fishing holes along Wappinger Creek. I absolutely looked both ways as I crossed the busy New Hackensack Road. Poor Puff. Poor Buff.

Poor Biff. Poor Willie. You can see why I have never developed close relationships with our cats while growing up. They had weird names, too. We named Willie after Wilcox Park where we found him.

As I walked down the hill, I could see our creek in the distance. Wow, I loved this creek. I missed this creek. As I got closer, something was different. That smell. What was that smell? Why was it so dirty? What was that brown foam floating around? Why was there garbage on the banks? All I could see were large two-foot-long carp. No other fish. As I lifted rocks by the rapids, I could not find one crawfish, which used to be readily available for fishing bait. All I could see was a rusty shopping cart laying in the mud and a bunch of beer cans.

It brought back memories from a few years earlier—April 22, 1970. I remembered exactly where I was—pulling old tires, a shopping cart, soda cans, and garbage out of the small stream in front of Roy C. Ketchum High School participating in the *very first* Earth Day with the newly formed high school club, PYE—Protect Your Environment. That was cool and everything, but I had not thought that our creek could have become that messed up, too.

The creek had died while I was away each summer camping at Wilcox Park. I was truly saddened. Since there are no coincidences in life, I will not tell you it was a coincidence that I found a copy of Rachel Carson's *Silent Spring* in my hands earlier that same year. I realized our little part of Wappinger Creek was connected to and impacted by other parts of our environment, and especially impacted by the activities of uncaring people. I am in awe that one person, one book, could raise environmental consciousness within the human condition. Now I really did wonder what was upstream.

It was late June and it had been a rainy week. I was going stir-crazy being stuck in the house for days as the remnants of Hurricane Agnes took a turn and traveled up the Hudson Valley as a tropical storm. Although western New York received much more flooding than we did, Wappinger Creek had peaked just below flood stage a few days earlier. That was always my invitation to check out the creek. I mean after every flood, just to make sure everything was okay and to see what treasures may have landed on the banks—usually a few good fishing lures—from upstream.

I was not disappointed as I walked along the rapids and scanned the usual flood-like debris. I came upon a big, rusty, tank-like structure sitting among the weeds where the high-water point of this week's tropical storm had peaked. I was afraid to lift it up by myself, so off I went to recruit Paul, Mike, and Jack, who eventually joined me in the investigation of the rusty structure. We turned it over carefully and determined it was a home heating fuel oil tank that had been cut in half lengthwise.

In our teenage wisdom, we dragged it back to Paul and Mike's house, where the creek was calmer, and put it in the water to see if it would float. The creek level was higher than normal, but the muddy flood waters had surrendered to a near-normal clear water flow.

While we held the oil tank still, Paul climbed in. Our newly discovered boat did float! This revelation led to an idea, which led to another, and another, and another. Soon we had cut the proper lengths of two-by-six boards to use as bench seats, located some old canoe paddles, and packed lunches. In the midday sun, we launched our rusty scupper from the wooden stairs where I first had been introduced to Wappinger Creek more than ten years earlier. We were on our way downstream—Paul and Jack navigated in front, while Mike and I were in the back. We paddled past the previous winter's ice hockey rink area and headed for the rapids, those same rapids that had eaten many hockey pucks. The carp didn't care that we were leaving, and our parents didn't know.

We navigated the first small rapids very effectively but realized the sheer weight of this heating oil tank (*ahem*) boat would require a keen awareness of what was ahead. You see, in all those years growing up as river rats, we never traveled downstream—much less set the goal to navigate the creek all the way to Wappinger Lake. We were ready for this adventure—or so we thought.

Eventually, we passed Rymph's Farm, the place where my mom had swum when she was our age. There was no one there. We discussed stopping, but the rope swing, still hanging from the old oak tree, looked frayed and tattered. Unsafe, I thought. The carp in this part of the creek didn't care that we decided not to stop. Besides, we had a long way to travel.

The next interesting stop along the way was the Dutchess County Airport. The creek flowed along the backside of the airport. On a nice, sunny day like this, we were likely to see an airplane take off. Maybe we would stop, climb the hill, and touch the end of the runway just for fun. We had forgotten that just before the airport was the Dutchess County Landfill. These were the days when landfills were not covered daily with soil, and birds would gather in the hundreds to eat the exposed garbage.

There was a stench in the air. *No stopping to eat lunch here*, I thought. As we approached this area, we could see the garbage being pushed over the hill and rolling toward the creek—washing machines, tires, grocery carts, paper, yuck! This is not the down-stream sights we were expecting. There was an orange liquid running out of the base of the landfill down the hill and right into our creek. Rachel Carson was right. We were ruining our own planet. I thought she was talking about somewhere else. People were ruining our own creek right here in Dutchess County.

I started to tell Paul, Mike, and Jack about the book I had finished reading, *Silent Spring*, and that I had decided to go to college and do that kind of science, you know—cleaning up our environment. We were still in shock staring at the orange liquid flowing into the creek as we turned the next bend in the river. We had momentarily forgotten that we were piloting an iron freighter. We should have been paying attention to where the current was taking us.

You see, the landfill dirt and garbage had narrowed the creek, causing the water current to speed up and become deeper.

We didn't see that just twenty feet ahead, a large maple tree had recently fallen across the entire creek. And we were heading straight for it. We tried to paddle toward the shore, but to no avail. Our rusty heating oil tank was moving at a pretty good clip, and we were about to hit our own proverbial iceberg, a massive tangle of maple tree branches still full of green leaves.

We all panicked. Someone yelled, "Bail out!" And we all jumped out of the boat just as it hit the horizontal tree trunk and branches that stretched across the whole creek. Unfortunately, I was the last to jump as the front of the boat hit the tree and went up in the air. The water current caught the back end and the boat flipped right on top of my legs. The current sucked the heavy rusty heating oil tank underneath the tree, dragging me down along with it. My legs were stuck under the oil tank, and I was well below the surface of the water in a rapidly moving Wappinger Creek.

I was trapped. I struggled to free my legs. I was really panicking. Adrenaline was fully flowing through my body. I flailed my arms around hoping to grab on to something and pull myself out, but I was too deep under the water. My long, brown hair was flowing wildly in my face. I had felt this panic before in my childhood dreams of drowning near the Red Oaks Mill falls. This time, I was not going to wake up safely tucked in my bed.

The weird thing about drowning, or maybe any near-death experience, is that time slows down. Maybe it's because senses heighten to another level. I'm not sure about any of that. I will simply tell you about my experience during the summer of '72—on that day—at that moment.

Yes, in that moment, I had clarity. I remembered my guardian angel, Nathaniel, was always with me. He was in my bedroom when I was only eight years old. He comforted me with his touch after my great-grandmother's death. He sent an angel to save Jack, Kevin, and me from our deaths in the baseball dugout collapse. He talked to me about a loving God last summer at Wilcox Park. My fear went away. My struggling ceased. I became very calm.

I turned toward the current and my long, brown hair flowed back off my face. The water felt like it was flowing in slow motion. It felt so good on my face, each molecule of water caressing my skin. I could hardly tell where my face ended, and Wappinger Creek began. Is this how it was to be? Would I die in peace in the creek that I so dearly loved?

In my mind I addressed God in prayer, "God, if this is my time to go, I am ready. But, if this is *not* my time, I really need your help!" I was so surprised, not that I received an immediate response, but what the message was in that moment. I heard a voice—the familiar voice of my guardian angel, Nathaniel—and he asked, "David, would you like to stay, or would you like to come with us?"

Wow. Wow! I had not considered that staying here or going *there* would be a choice. I had only expressed my heartfelt and sincere thought that I would be at peace with God's decision regarding my life. I ignored the pesky fact my legs were still trapped under a rusty oil tank under a maple tree at the bottom of a rapidly flowing and deep Wappinger Creek. I had a decision to make. I was quite sure that whatever I decided, so it would be.

I know that, as you read this, it is truly hard to believe that all my flailing, struggling, thoughts, memories, interactions, and thoughtful decisions about my own life or death could have possibly occurred in the very short time I had been holding my breath. Although time does slow down, it was certainly beneficial playing hold-your-breath games at Wilcox Park all summer for years. But still, I knew I had to decide quickly. My family was a consideration, but I finally decided to stay for one reason—Rachel Carson's book *Silent Spring*. She had shown me there was work to be done. Our creek, where I could apparently choose to die in, was already dead. My thoughts were crystal clear—to not cause any confusion on their part about my desire—I thought clearly, *I will stay here so I can help clean up the environment in this world.*

Instantaneously, a hand grabbed my arm just below my left wrist. I was pulled hard enough to free my legs from the rusty oil tank. I could feel the skin on the back of my calves ripping as I was freed. My left hand was placed on a branch above the surface, and I used my remaining strength to pull my head out of the water. I gasped for a breath. I glanced in all directions for the person who had pulled me from the water. Paul? Mike? Jack? But no one was there. I was alone. Well, not really. I mean to say I was surrounded only by love. I smiled and said aloud, "Thank you, God."

About fifty yards downstream, where the creek widened back to its original size, I could see Paul, Mike, and Jack standing in knee-deep water. The oil tank resurfaced on the downstream side of the maple tree and was upside down floating toward them. I waved and they waved back. I crawled along the tree trunk to the bank of the creek. It felt good to get on solid ground. As I approached, they yelled, "Hey, where were you? We thought you drowned." I stated matter-of-factly, "I thought so too. I was stuck under the tree." One of the guys suggested we stop our journey. "When will we ever have the chance to do this again? Let's go on," I urged.

The unspoken thought on my part was that in a couple years, I was leaving for college to become an environmental scientist, just like Rachel Carson. We flipped over the oil tank and transformed it back into a boat to discover what was in store for the rest of our travels.

As we floated downstream in the now calm current, the wind caressed my face as it was warmed by the afternoon sun. The sky was the bluest I'd ever seen. Every bird that chirped sounded new. The rest of our trip down Wappinger Creek was thankfully uneventful—peaceful even. I was glad that I had decided to stay on this Earth, even if it could possibly be for only one more day or for thirty thousand more days. Because how do we really know?

When I see a blue sky or appreciate the feeling of the wind gracing my face, I think of that day. The day I chose to stay here on Earth. The day we dreamed of traveling downstream. Four boys. One creek. *Thank you, God. Thank you, Nathaniel. Thank you, Rachel Carson.*

A Spiritual Perspective on Choice

At the time

As I lifted myself out of the water and gasped for air, I felt like I was being born again—maybe a baptism of sorts. I was given a great gift—the gift of choice—to continue this life path or to change directions into the next existence. As we continued down-stream that day, I just knew I would fulfill my destiny to stay and help clean up Mother Earth. My choice.

As I write today

First off, I will address the obvious question. Did I continue my path of cleaning up the environment as promised? On Friday, May 9, 1980, I accepted my award as the American Chemical Society, New York Chapter top college-graduating chemist during the commencement ceremony at State University of New York (SUNY), College of Environmental Science and Forestry, where I graduated Magna Cum Laude in Environmental Analytical Chemistry. Not coincidentally, I did my Senior Independent Study project on the treatment of landfill leachate, the orange liquid flowing into our creek on the day I almost drowned. Nan and Pop even traveled to my college graduation—the first college graduate in our family's history.

And yes, after graduation, I spent twenty years as an environmental chemist analyzing and cleaning up industrial toxic waste—in streams, ditches, underground, on top of the ground, in storage tanks, in groundwater, dumped in the back forty, accidentally spilled—PCBs, toluene, acetone, styrene, lead, arsenic, waste oil, cutting oil, transformer oil, transmission oil, and a whole host of other cancer-causing chlorinated hydrocarbons. I traveled the country cleaning up industrial chemical messes in California, Colorado, Florida, Georgia, Illinois, Indiana, Kentucky, Maryland, Michigan, New Jersey, New York, Ohio, Pennsylvania, Texas, and West Virginia. When my journey as an environmental chemist was finally over, I felt that I had done my part—as I had promised to God and to Nathaniel in the summer of 1972.

When I recount my near-drowning experience to others, I always end with, "I am here on Earth in *chosen time*." I use this phrase because I not only chose to come here to this earthly existence, but when given the option, I also chose to stay. The Church of Jesus Christ of Latter-Day Saints believes that before we arrive in our physical bodies in this earthly existence, we are God's angel children in Heaven, fully aware sentient spirits choosing to come to Earth for the purpose of soul growth. I believe that to be true.

My story is not unique, as many people have had near-death experiences, even further along that transitional path than I, and have chosen to come back to this earthly dimension, maybe for love of their family, maybe to complete some unfinished business, or mend relationships. More often though, people who recount near-death experiences tell of loved ones on the other side of the veil saying to them in a loving manner, "It is not your time yet, but we will be here when it is."

This is a good time to discuss life-path choices. Life-path choices are those moments when our present life path potentially branches off into alternate journeys, alternate possibilities, and/or alternate realities on our personal tree of life. I'm not referencing the daily decisions like what to have for dinner, which way to drive home, or whether I wear blue or green today. Those decisions are deeply embedded into our free-will, daily lives. I'm referring to the two, three, or four decisions that completely changed the course of your life. Those are the major branches on your tree of life. You know what yours are. Your life-altering choices.

We all arrive in this time-space dimension with a soul plan we have created. If we choose to adhere to our personally constructed blueprint, these pre-arranged plans will lead us into situations that enhance our spiritual growth. But remember, we are still blessed with free will. Each one of us may just allow the flow of life to take us randomly toward whatever experience is next—like a jellyfish riding the currents of an ever-changing ocean tide. And that's okay. That path can be adventurous! Or filled with unexpected trials and tribulations. Or both.

It is also okay to change or modify your soul plan by living your life with *intention*. Intention being a thought, spoken aloud, and acted upon, sending information to the Universal energy that we are ready to change direction. Maybe even leave this existence at the next life exit ramp opportunity, or merely to continue in this time-space dimension, but on a different path. Our life's journey is always in formation. Are you a co-manifesting participant?

I'll expand upon my experiences from this chapter. What if I chose to leave this Earth when I was drowning in Wappinger Creek? I feel as if it was one of my pre-arranged life-exit options, but I chose not to experience that opportunity. If I hadn't read Rachel Carson's *Silent Spring* just weeks before, things might have been different. What if I wasn't angry about the polluted orange leachate spewing from the landfill garbage into the creek? What if I had sat on the front seat of the rusty tank instead of the back? In the end, none of those questions mattered because I had a relationship with God. I chose to have a connection with my guardian angel, Nathaniel. And in my life, that's what has made all the difference.

A few years back, I had a waking dream—a vision really. I was shown a diagram of how we transition through critical-decision branches on our own tree of life. For example, as you approach a time in your life when multiple paths present themselves—one may change your life, one may maintain the status quo, or maybe even send you toward a painful lesson. In all cases, it is *your* path to choose. But how does an involved Universe energetically prepare the way for your future free-will choice?

Intent. As you approach an important branching of your life path, the Universe takes its cue from your thoughts, words, and actions—in other words, y*our intent*. The Universe of guardian angels, guides, master teachers, and God will place people, messages, and coincidences in your path to gauge your intent.

Why would the Universe want to gauge your intent? Because they are preparing a path ahead based upon your potential future free-will choice options. When you send mixed signals, constantly flip-flopping your intent, you will create a rougher journey toward your destination. The clearer you are in your intent, the smoother the path will be laid out for you. Truly, the Universe will lay out the red carpet when your intent aligns with your highest good—your soul plan. It may even seem like it was *destiny* because it went so smoothly.

At critical moments in your life, it's your free-will choice to decide which life path to take. Don't be afraid—just think it, speak it, act on it. It's not selfish. It's not self-centered. *It's centered in self.* Choose to be centered within yourself.

Finding Clarity:
> *Am I able to center myself and manifest a life path*
> *that is for my highest good?*

Living with joy and incorporating only-love in our lives may be the most difficult challenge for each of us traveling on this planet at this time in history. An overarching reason we came here is to contrast, compare, and define what is *only-love*—so that we may understand God. Only-love doesn't know the completeness of only-love until it is contrasted with what is not-love.

Allow me to clarify. . . what if every human being grew to measure exactly seventy-two inches from head-to-toe? The concept of height—*tallness or shortness*—would not be in our conscious awareness. We can only appreciate being tall when in comparison to being short, and vice versa. By filtering and sifting through our life choices, and our perceptions of the world around us, we can become more aware of what is not-love and realize the fullness of only-love—God's love. Then we may awaken to our true nature as beings of light and love.

Once awake, we must take every opportunity to pray that love will overcome darkness. That humanity will make a collective life-path course correction—together. Bless those who shine a light of love on situations of not-love. Pray for the spiritual warriors. Even from the sidelines, we can all make a difference. It's time to wake up.

Human history is measured and filled with choices of not-love and choices of only-love. Allow me to point out some historical examples of not-love, and the resulting only-love reactions, through my own perspective:

- *The purging of "undesirable" Jews, blacks, and disabled people by Hitler's fascist Nazi Germany was a clear example of not-love. What you may or may not realize is that most of the world's leaders allowed the Nazis to implement genocide for years before there was any movement to stop it. Even in America at the time, our politicians ignored that the German government had created holding camps for any citizen who was deemed undesirable—those who didn't agree with the growing fascist Nazi movement. In the meanwhile, the citizens were unaware of this evil.*

Ultimately, this historical event provided the aware souls—those awake to the evil—an opportunity to personally express only-love, as documented in the historical books and movies *Schindler's List*, *The Diary of Anne Frank*, *Saving Private Ryan*, *The Sound of Music*, and *The Red Tails*, just to name a few. When the world is exhibiting not-love, be the soul that chooses only-love. I am certain that thousands of only-love miracles remain undocumented.

- *Let's move across the Atlantic Ocean to the internment camps in America. Did you know? According to the website,* History.com, *"Through Executive Order 9006, Japanese internment camps were established [in the United States] during World War II by President Franklin D. Roosevelt." There was a total of ten prison camps—called Relocation Centers—where anyone who was of at least one-sixteenth Japanese descent was forcibly taken from their homes by the United States government. And more than two-thirds of those incarcerated people were American citizens.*

At the time, Attorney General Francis Biddle pleaded with the president that mass incarceration was not necessary. He was attempting to implement only-love in the face of political pressure and fear. According to *History.com*, "Roosevelt signed the order anyway." Most Americans were unaware of these terrible actions. For more information, visit the resources of the Japanese American National Museum at *janm.org*.

We have plenty of opportunities to formulate these definitions for ourselves. And that's the conundrum. It is very challenging in a world full of not-love to live with peace in our hearts and joy in our souls. It is difficult to watch as God's children are damaged by life. Damaged by not-love. Although it gives each of us an opportunity to exhibit only-love.

Start or end each day with a prayer or say a prayer before eating dinner—it's your choice—specifically to manifest only-love in a world still engulfed in the not-love darkness. Thank the Universe (God, Jesus, your guardian angels, universal energy, Holy Spirit, the Ascended Masters—it's all connected) for all your blessings. Be open to all information, choices, insights, thoughts, and actions that will lead you to co-manifest the best version of our world within a collective consciousness of only-love. Manifest joy for yourself. Spiritual warriors need joy, too! And when you inject joy into your life and mix it with focused intent, you are unstoppable. Collectively, we are unstoppable.

Daily Affirmation

I journey through life with informed choices and clear intent.

"Intuition is the whisper of the soul."

~Jiddu Krishnamurti, Philosopher and Author

Chapter Seven

Riding Shotgun

A Spiritual Perspective on Intuition

Flotsam and Jetson

David K. Munson ©2022

I float aimlessly like a jellyfish
through the ebb and flow
of the ocean tides.

Not unlike the flotsam and jetson
of my discarded life choices.

As if by random chance,
a moment of joy intersects my path.

Intuitively, I choose to accept this blessing
as a gift from a loving Universe.
I am not alone.
I am changed.

It was so weird stepping on the mound to pitch as I nervously twirled the ball in my hand. I looked over at the bench, as usual, but my dad was not there. He had been my coach for every Little League and Junior League baseball game I had played since I was eight years old. Today, Coach S. was there—the catcher's dad who I had just met moments ago. My world had changed in an instant.

A few days earlier, my dad had packed up his clothes and left—for a new life. And apparently, that meant leaving as coach of our Junior League baseball team, too. I was glad my cousin Jack was playing shortstop today. I don't remember much about the weeks that followed, or the rest of that baseball season. I spent a lot of time outside because I just couldn't listen to my mom crying all the time and so out-of-it on pills as to be mostly non-functional. My mom didn't work outside the home, so we had no income, and the neighbors and relatives had stopped bringing food weeks ago. We were getting hungry.

At some point, Karen and I took Mom's pills and flushed them down the toilet. No more pills! We followed that up with re-minding her we were just teenagers. She was the adult, so she needed to get it together. We were too young to officially work, although we mowed lawns, shoveled snow for neighbors, and babysat to earn extra money to help pay the bills.

Eventually, things settled into a dysfunctional normalcy. My mom got a job cleaning rich peoples' houses for under-the-table cash.

Our future stepfather had already moved into our house. I got my learner's permit to drive. It was the time of my split personality. Honor student and baseball player during the day. In the evenings and weekends—well, they were filled with smoking cigarettes, smoking pot, and drinking alcohol to numb the pain. It was easy living this double life, as no adult was paying attention.

Many summer nights I would sneak out of my house, by climbing down the porch from the second floor, to meet Mike. We would go to Macghee Park, smoke a joint, and lay on the blacktop of the street, still warm from the day's summer sun, and stare at the stars. Some nights we would lay there quietly and enjoy the beauty of the Milky Way. Other nights we would lament about the latest girl who would not return our affections. We always talked and cried with each other. I would say, "The right girl is out there for each of us," just like I was told earlier sitting on that log in Wilcox Park.

My goals were simple: get good enough grades so that I can go to college without getting arrested for smoking pot. I had developed a whole new set of strategies for surviving the next two years of high school. And that's when Nathaniel started interacting in my life more frequently.

In school, I felt like an outcast—the shy, long-haired student who was in honors with the nerds. Outside of school, the pot-smoking freaks at parties would ask why a brainiac like me was hanging out with this crowd. Same as them, I suppose. Just trying to forget about life for a while—and yes, that's a Billy Joel song lyric. I was balancing my exit strategy—not a life-exit, but an escape from an abusive, alcoholic stepfather and a mom who was too damaged to stop it, or fix it.

Every time my daily life transitioned from nerdy high school honor student to long-haired hippy pot-smoking freak, I would say a prayer for protection, "Please God, protect us all from trouble so that I can escape this house, go to college, and become the person I promised when you saved me from drowning." I know that may sound strange to most people, because the easiest answer would have been to just stop smoking pot and partying. But that was the only part of our lives that dulled the pain.

The early days of partying seemed fun and carefree—smoking pot, drinking Boone's Farm apple wine, and lots of laughing. Laughing as we partied on the bleachers of our baseball field at Macghee Park, in the basements of friends' houses, in the woods with a bonfire, in Mike's car—and that's where this story goes.

We all piled into Mike's 1968 green four-door Chevy Impala. That car was a sturdy tank and could easily fit six teenagers—including my sister, Karen, and cousin, Jack, for a fun joy ride on a sunny Saturday afternoon with nowhere to go. We had already smoked a joint and were heading east on New Hackensack Road just past George's Supermarket, right before the Dutchess County Airport where the landfill had impacted the creek.

Over the blasting music of The Allman Brothers *Eat a Peach* 8-track, I heard Nathaniel yell at me, "David, grab the steering wheel!" Well, I was sitting in the back seat and didn't know what to do. I didn't even have my learners permit yet. So just in case, I leaned forward—we didn't wear seat belts at the time—and put my hand on the front seat between Mike and Karen while everyone continued to sing *Ramblin' Man.* I'm not sure why or how, but the Chevy Impala drifted to the right, hit the uneven shoulder, and jerked the car toward the guard rail. You know, the guard rail that theoretically would prevent a car full of stoned teenagers from going over the two-hundred-foot cliff into Wappinger Creek. I was ready and reacted quickly. I reached between my sister and Mike, grabbed the steering wheel, and jerked it back onto New Hackensack Road just as we grazed the guard rail. My role in our new party world changed that day from a carefree participant to an on-alert protector.

The warnings would start to come more frequently. One day, it was my turn to ride in the front passenger seat. I was fully aware that a carload of long-haired high school kids in the mid-1970s was an invitation for a cop to stop us and search for pot. That was exactly the trouble I was praying wouldn't happen.

Out of nowhere, a voice said, "David, there is a police car around this turn." I looked at Mike, who was driving, and said, "Slow down. There's a cop around this turn." I turned to the backseat where Paul and Jack were sitting and implored "Duck down, now!" I quickly tucked my long hair into my baseball cap just as we passed by the cop—going the speed limit, two normal-looking boys with baseball caps—and an ounce of pot in the backseat. Enough to send us all to jail. Two important lessons were available to me that day: my guardian angel was always with me even when I was *not* about to die; and never carry more drugs with you than you need for that specific outing.

Over the next few months, I would get warnings from my guardian angel, Nathaniel. *There's a policeman around the next turn* was a common warning, which entitled me to ride shotgun most of the time. Paul, Mike, and Jack learned to heed my warnings, too.

As we drove up to attend a large neighborhood party, I heard the message, *be careful,* so I suggested that we park the car on the next street over—away from the party. As we entered the house, all the freaks and drinkers were already quite rowdy. I scoped out the backyard fence as a possible escape option, informed my peeps that if trouble started, we could jump the back fence and get right to where our car was parked. I wasn't surprised when the party started to get out of hand and the police arrived. We all implemented the escape plan, jumped the fence, ran through the neighbor's yard, and drove off safely—well out of view of the police. From that time on, I always had a safe escape plan—no matter where the party was—and it served us well more than once.

I continued to listen for Nathaniel's voice foretelling of danger ahead and implemented different survival strategies to stay out of trouble. I utilized my smarts to minimize the possibility of getting arrested for doing something stupid that would draw attention to us from the authorities. The most important strategy was travel in the car with only a few rolled joints—we could swallow them quickly if the need arose. So, I became an expert joint roller. Also, never ever carry a pot pipe in the car because it's too hard to hide, and any observant police officer would see us throw it out the window. Sometimes, we would use an apple to smoke pot, because we could always eat the apple as the officer searched the car. There were many other strategies, but suffice it to say, I was a control freak trying to protect our futures.

If the party was at our house, we always ended the party at least an hour before our parents were expected home. That gave us enough time for proper and thorough clean-up and airing out of the house by opening every window. There were certainly close calls with police and with dangerous situations. I suppose trouble and danger are relative terms. It seems things are much more dangerous in America now than in the 1970s—drugs laced with fentanyl, much stronger pot, meth labs, gangs, illegal guns, human trafficking, and shootings. Being in the wrong place at the wrong time was not as dangerous back then.

As time went on, I got my driver's license, and I had use of a gold 1964 Rambler American station wagon. I felt safe driving that car back and forth to my after-school and summer job at W. T. Grants Department Store. It looked like a family vehicle, and if you floored the gas pedal it would max out at only 55 mph! Besides my long, brown hair flying in the wind while blasting Jimi Hendrix's *All Along the Watchtower* on my newly installed speakers, there was never a reason for a cop to pull me over.

What was W. T. Grants you might ask? Well, before filing bankruptcy in 1976, it was the largest retailer in the United States, much like Woolworths or today's Walmart stores. I started there at age fifteen as the candy department salesclerk to help Mom with the finances, save some money for college, put gas in the Rambler for thirty-six cents per gallon, and buy a little bit of pot, not necessarily in that order.

Soon, I was the candy department manager—a dubious honor at the time since every other department in the store was losing money. I had no direct reports, and none of the other Grants' employees wanted to manage the candy department. I found my own voice while implementing changes to the Grants' corporate office directives, which dictated to every store exactly how to sell candy. I figured if they were that smart, why couldn't they make money selling candy—which everyone loves! I managed the candy department based upon the actions and inputs from customers, not what the stuffy suits in the ivory tower said.

I had become aware that Nathaniel was not only there to warn me of danger but to guide me in inspirational ways, too. For example, I was so annoyed every Saturday when mothers and their kids would be standing in line at the cash registers—with the kids whining and crying. I was very judgmental about that situation, so I prayed for some inspirational guidance—mostly to reduce my annoyance. I received a suggestion from Nathaniel and pitched the idea to management. The W.T. Grants location on Route 44 in Poughkeepsie became the very first store, that I am aware of, to stock candy bars on both sides of the check-out lines, replacing the usual boring batteries, thread, hand cream, etc. It was a very successful way to sell additional candy, as most moms reached for it to shut up their kids. It was more work for me, but I revamped the corporate ordering strategies to fit this change.

Within a few months, I managed the only department in that store location that was showing a profit. It didn't hurt either that each holiday, I reduced the recommended ordering quantities for candy corn and spiced jelly beans, reduced the recommended ordering quantities for marshmallow Peeps at Easter, increased the ordering of Reese's Peanut Butter cups and Snickers—and put them on end caps contrary to the corporate dictates. At sixteen, I felt like I had a partner helping to inspire me and to keep me out of trouble, when necessary. A guardian angel riding shotgun.

I remember a few times when I did *not* listen to Nathaniel's warning voice in my head—I'll call them the *ice storm incident* and the *lying Harold fiasco*.

I'll start with the *ice storm incident*. It was a wintery weekend, and the weather was bad. Those were the hardest days living in a dysfunctional household because it was like you were locked in a mental institution and just wanted to escape. On that Saturday, instead of snow, we were getting a rare ice storm. Everything outside was coated with a thick layer of ice. We were bound and determined to make our escape in my Rambler station wagon, so out the door we went against the weather warnings from our mom. I wanted to get out of the house so badly that I even closed my mind to any potential warning from Nathaniel. My sisters, cousin Jack, and I made quick work of scraping the ice off the car windows and out of the driveway we drove to pick up some friends—especially Deanna, who I had a secret crush on for many years.

She lived at the Garden Apartments—the ones Kevin, Jack, and I rode our bikes past a few years earlier to steal candy from George's Supermarket. I insisted Deanna sit in the front seat next to me as I drove. I liked the smell of her long, straight, blonde hair. I loved the memories of playing kick the can in our backyard together years earlier. I loved the memories of watching her play softball, athletically running to first base with her blonde hair shimmering in the summer sun at Macghee Park.

But today, it wasn't sunny at all—just very icy on the roads. As we picked up Deanna, I promised her mom I would drive carefully—and I sincerely meant that. As we turned right, out of the Garden Apartments onto Maloney Road, the hill stretching down toward New Hackensack Road seemed steeper than usual—especially covered with ice that had not yet been salted. I was braking to take the hill slowly—much slower than on my forest green one-speed bike! We began to pick up speed on the ice and the Rambler's brakes were not holding. Suddenly, I saw a vision in my eyes—like someone placed a virtual reality headset on me—of our car sliding across New Hackensack Road right into the gas pumps of the Shell station and exploding. Before I could react, I heard *her* voice. My female guardian angel. My protector. If she was here, then we must be in life-altering danger.

"Turn your wheel to the left, now!" she demanded. I looked left and all that was there was a deep ditch, but I did not hesitate. I jerked the wheel to the left. The Rambler just kept sliding straight down the steep Maloney Road hill right towards that Shell station. A few seconds later, the front tires must have gained enough traction somehow and jolted to the left directly into the parking lot entrance of George's Supermarket.

As we entered the icy parking lot, we started into a 360-degree spin. Deanna's long, blonde hair was flying around the front seat as we completed multiple rotations in the empty parking lot. When the vehicle finally stopped rotating, we started to gain our bearings. The concrete base of a parking lot light pole was just inches outside my driver's door. I looked to the right to see all the loop-de-loops our car had completed. *How did we ever miss all those other light poles in our path?* We sat there in silence for what seemed like minutes. "Oh my God, we were lucky," Deanna said, still in a state of shock. "Let's go home," I said. We all got out of the car and walked back up Maloney Road hill to ensure Deanna got home safely, as I had promised her mom.

Now for the *lying Harold fiasco*. We were partying at Paul and Mike's house with a small group of friends when the local drug dealer, Harold, showed up. That wasn't a regular occurrence, so my internal radar was on high alert. Things were going fine until someone decided we should all go up to Red Oaks Mill for pizza, something we did on a regular basis. And the pizzeria owner didn't mind if we were high, as long as we didn't cause trouble.

Nathaniel's warning occurred after Harold offered to drive all of us to the pizza parlor, because his car was blocking the driveway. Everyone, except me, was cool with that idea. I asked Harold directly, "I'm good with going, as long as we are all clean and there's no pot in the car." He assured me that all was good, so I got in the back seat. There I was—in the car of the biggest drug dealer in the county—at midnight on a Saturday with a bunch of stoned and hungry teenagers.

As we approached the pizzeria in Red Oaks Mill, the red and blue flashing lights of the Sheriff's squad car filled the spaces in our vehicle. I was glad I had confirmed with Harold that we were not carrying drugs with us on our pizza run. Harold pulled his car over and said, "Everyone be cool. But I have a pound of pot in the trunk under the spare tire." That was enough to label all of us drug dealers, sending us all to jail for a long time.

As the officers approached the car with their flashlights and asked us to get out, so many emotions came over me at that moment—anger, fear, mad at myself for not listening to Nathaniel's warning just minutes earlier. As we all stood there under the streetlights, one of the Sheriffs told Harold to open the trunk. As the Sheriff shined his flashlight right at the spare tire, I said a prayer from the deepest part of my soul, "Dear God, I thought I was protecting everyone. I'm scared. Please help us avoid being arrested for something we did not do." Obviously, I wasn't referring to Harold.

At that instant—at midnight on a Saturday in little Red Oaks Mill—two loud Harley Davidson chopper motorcycles appeared out of nowhere racing right past the Sheriff's vehicle with the red and blue lights still flashing. They were dressed in black leather with long hair flying in the wind and their arms reaching high onto their ape-hanger handlebars. As they sped past us, they yelled something at the two Sheriffs who were about to discover the stash in Harold's trunk.

Both Sheriffs stopped what they were doing, jumped back into their squad car, and raced down New Hackensack Road chasing after the choppers. "What the f**k!" I yelled at Harold. "You were lying, a$$hole. I specifically asked if you had any pot in the car. And you said no." Mike interjected, "Calm down, it all worked out, so let's get back in the car and go get pizza." I stated very clearly, "There is no f**king way I'm getting back in Harold's car ever again."

And I walked home—all by myself—promising I would never again ignore warnings of any type. A voice from the sky. A voice in my head. An invisible tap on my shoulder. Or just plain gut intuition.

As my high school days were winding down, I would take the time to walk up to East Bend Lake and lay down in a field of tall grass where no one could find me. My escape from this dysfunctional household was imminent, and I was thankful. I was thankful for that strong female voice that only came during those occasions when my life was in imminent danger. I was especially thankful for Nathaniel—his voice coming into my consciousness from the left side of my head—who had been my constant companion on my life's journey.

I felt I should say thank you to him, so I did—in my head and aloud. I heard a response, "You're welcome, David." I didn't have to ask who it was. I had heard that voice many, many times in my life, especially over the past few years navigating through high school. I smiled. "Will you be with me at college?" I asked. "Yes, of course. We have been together from before you were born into this world.

And I will be with you always." Wow. Wow. That's a lot to process. My guardian angel, Nathaniel, has been with me the whole time as I wandered through this life.

A Spiritual Perspective on Intuition

At the time

I felt blessed. I grew from being a scared little boy asking God a question in my bedroom, to a teenager interacting with my guardian angel, Nathaniel. And having angels save my life at least three times—that I was even aware of.

This knowledge gave me the strength to realize I would be okay leaving for college. My sisters, Karen, and Sue, both moved to Florida to get out of the house. I would miss them. I would miss my cousin, Jack, who was going into the military. I would miss my best friends, Paul, and Mike, too.

Intuitively, I knew I was on the threshold of a major life change. I discovered that loneliness is only a state of mind—an incomplete sense of reality. And I knew I would never be alone.

As I write today

This may be the hardest—or maybe the easiest—section to write. There are thousands of examples in my life where intuitive messages have helped me—when Nathaniel intervened to give me a message. Or events were swayed to deliver my highest good or my greatest life lesson. Even daily tasks, that might seem mundane, seemed to be blessed by a loving Universe. I will state this simple truth: everything and everyone can easily connect with the Universe through aware intent—thoughts, spoken aloud, and acted upon. For clarification purposes, guardian angels, or any entity, cannot read our thoughts without our permission. They must gauge our intent through our spoken words and actions. Mixed messages are common.

To make our relationship closer, I gave Nathaniel permission to know my thoughts and understand my mind. He no longer had to guess what my intent was based on hearing my spoken words or observing my actions. He had a front-row seat to all my free-will thoughts—my intent. And I know he would act only if it was for my soul's highest good. He already understood my heart. At some point in my life, I realized Nathaniel already knew why I came to this time-space reality on Earth during the millennium transition toward The Golden Age of only-love.

I also have learned if your life is stuck, or you are unhappy, *clear the clutter*. Let me clarify—dump the drama. Remove the people in your life who cause you emotional and/or physical upset.

Finding Clarity:
> *Am I able to clear the emotional and/or physical drama holding me captive in the present?*

Start a plan to move on [*from that job, relationship, house, co-worker, relative, friend, social media site*] and begin to implement it—because the alternative is that the Universe will take you out of that situation sooner or later for your own highest good. It's much less stressful if you act as a co-creator of your own destiny rather than being strewn about like the proverbial jellyfish—unless you relish playing the victim. Or you like uncomfortable surprises.

New life-path options are out there for you! But these opportunities can't emerge through the clutter and obstacles that our egos have placed in the way. So, you must get out of your own way. You merely have to open your heart and mind to your inherent intuition.

Bless others on their journeys too because that blessing will come back into your own life. Help others because that help will come back to you, too. Be fully present to accept intuition, coincidences, messages, and strangers who arrive in your life—they are there for a reason. Thank the Universe for all the blessings that are about to arrive. Live a life of gratitude. Live a life connected to the unseen, benevolent forces in our Universe.

Spirit wants you to experience the life circumstances and lessons you came here for. Thank the Universe for your experiences, even what might have appeared to be bad at the time. Truly, they want you to be happy. Be grateful—and full of great!

Daily Affirmation

I open my awareness to receive intuition in all its forms.

"I tell you the truth. If anyone says to this mountain, 'Go, throw yourself into the sea, and does not doubt in his heart but believes that what he says will happen, it will be done for him. Therefore, I tell you, whatever you ask for in prayer, believe that you have received it, and it will be yours."

~ ***Holy Bible KJV*;** **Mark 11:23-24**

Chapter Eight

Lost and Found

A Spiritual Perspective on Prayer

I Forgot to Talk to God

David K. Munson ©2021

Living life with dazed eyes.
Trudging through quicksand,
Only awakened with speed.
I forgot to talk to God.

Living life with a veiled heart.
Balancing through duality,
Only hoping to bleed.
I forgot to talk to God.

Living life with a chaotic mind.
Wandering through a maze,
Only quieted with weed.
I forgot to talk to God.

Living life with a graceful soul.
Lifted through prayer,
Instantly with angelic heed.
I remembered.

I screamed in my head, *what's going on?* as someone was grabbing at my t-shirt collar and shaking me out of a groggy Saturday morning sleep-in after a late Friday night of college partying. Before my eyes opened, all I could hear was a female voice saying, "David, wake up! This is not your life. Wake up!" The voice was certainly not one of my roommates, as I was living alone. I opened my eyes to see who was in my bedroom shaking me out of my slumber—*and why wasn't this my life*?

All I could see was a white, glistening, ethereal body hovering about two feet above me. She continued to shake my body by the collar of my t-shirt. Once again, I heard "David, this is not your life! You must wake up!" Although I had never actually seen an angel in my life, I recognized the voice of this angel who had saved my life years earlier in the third-base dugout at Macghee Park. That seemed so long ago—before my parent's divorce. Before my double life as an honors high school student, as I hid the messed-up teenager who was living on the proverbial razor-thin edge of trouble.

Some three years later, all I could say to this angel was, "I AM awake. Stop shaking me!" Suddenly, my head fell back onto the pillow, as the force that had gripped my t-shirt collar had let go—and her presence was gone. I laid there for quite a while. Her words resonated in my head—*this is not your life.*

Well, let's take an inventory, I thought. I am on my mattress on the floor of my bedroom in an apartment on top of a hill in Oneonta, NY.

I am a junior at SUNY Oneonta. My room is a mess. There is not a textbook in sight. I thought I should get up, get dressed, and check out the apartment to be sure this was my life. Sure enough, the bong was on the coffee table next to the deck of cards from a game of Crazy Eights the night before. My friends and I loved to play cards to pass the time when we were not hiking the Catskills.

My refrigerator was bare—only the saltines, peanut butter, and pasta were in the cupboards. I knew not to look in the freezer, but I did anyway. I was hoping for a miracle that there might be meat in there. Nope. My angel was here to tell me this wasn't my life, not to deliver meat, which I hadn't eaten in months. This was my life alright—and I hated it.

I'm going to go for a walk, I thought, as I turned to go out the apartment door into the gray morning. I walked down the hill with no destination in mind. I barely noticed the cold rain falling on this Saturday morning in November 1977—the last weekend before Thanksgiving. My mind was spinning with what had just occurred in my bedroom earlier that morning. Over and over in my head went the words, *this is not your life*.

Eventually, I ended up in Wilbur Park, where I had never walked to before, just down the hill from my apartment. I looked around for a picnic shelter and settled for sitting on the swings. I was already soaked from the rain anyway, although I was not in the mood to swing. There were more pressing matters.

Quite honestly, I had not reflected on my life in a long time. I was certain she did not mean I was living someone else's life—so her intended meaning must be that I was not on the right track with my present life path. How was my life going you may ask? Terribly. I was failing all my classes in this first semester of my junior year—a slight exaggeration—because I thought I might have a D in third semester Organic Chemistry.

This semester, I had only bothered to attend a handful of my 8:00 a.m. Differential Equations classes. I had spent way more time smoking pot, playing card games, pinball, foosball, and hiking alone in the mountains around campus than I did in all my classes combined. On some days, I would wake up and get dressed with every intention of going to class, but embarrassment would set in because I hadn't been to class in so long. I would then give up and smoke a joint to bury my feelings. Some days it worked—I just felt empty, which was better than feeling lost, alone, inadequate. On weekends, I would take the most recently available amphetamine, and "speed" through the hills, forests, cliffs, and bogs of upstate New York. I was killing time, if not myself.

Financially, I was also a wreck. I had been paying my own way through college—with loans and summer jobs. Now in the middle of my junior year, I was feeling the financial effects of making virtually no money the prior summer. Unfortunately, last summer, I was homeless. My alcoholic stepfather had kicked me out of the house just weeks after my sophomore year. He was mad because I wouldn't go back to Grants Department Store to work in the candy department for the summer, and jobs were hard to find that year.

He didn't know I wouldn't go back to Grants because my work friends—who were my co-workers at Grants for years—had formed a merchandise theft ring while I was gone and wanted me to come back to Grants to help them that summer. I would not do that—my life was already a mess—and I didn't want to go to jail. So, I had no job *and* no place to live. That seemed like a small price to pay compared to going to jail for theft.

So, this past summer, I slept in friends' basements for a few weeks, working temporary Manpower jobs on Long Island each day. Some days I organized scrap metal at small machine shops. For a few days, I organized and categorized all the warehouse inventory used throughout the year to decorate Macy's Department Store windows on 5th Avenue. I worked in a factory that canned institutional-sized cans of peanut butter. And on many days, I landscaped with different crews. Eventually, I was able to land a steady job as a camp counselor in Connecticut. It didn't pay much, but at least I had a tent over my head and three camp meals a day.

Most nights at college, I went to bed just so I didn't have to think about how hungry I was. My diet consisted mostly of ketchup on pasta or peanut butter and jelly on saltines. I clearly remember a moment in time—standing in front of the steaks in Price Chopper supermarket without a dime in my pocket. I was so hungry I seriously considered putting that steak under my big bulky winter coat and walking out of the store. I wouldn't even steal a Butterfinger at George's Supermarket when I was ten—but there I stood. That's how hungry I was. I struggled with how low I had fallen to consider stealing food. I didn't steal the steak—only because if I was caught, I was not sure if there was anyone in my life who cared enough to bail me out. So, I went hungry for another night.

I had also buried my heart. I had not yet healed from a breakup more than a year earlier with the first love of my life. I met her on the first day of college. I could always see spending the rest of my life with her. I missed her so much. Many days, I would be walking on campus and instead of going to class, I would randomly walk around just hoping to run into her—just for a moment—hoping a spark would be renewed. I would once again miss class. I felt so alone as I chased a dream that was not to be.

As I sat on that swing in that cold November rain, inventorying the status of my life—no money, no food, broken heart, pot smoker, and doing drugs to hide the pain—it was no surprise that I was also failing out of college. I hated my life. I HATED my life!

So, I guess this morning's angel encounter was about changing my life. "*Wake up. This is not your life*" is what I heard—and now it seemed more like a warning. I knew from my past that if an angel came into my life, if only for a moment, then I must listen. I must change my life now. But where would I start?

I decided to think back to the last time I was happy, and when it all changed. That seemed logical, and maybe I could reset the clock—reset my life. So, I started.

Hmmm—September 1974: I arrived at SUNY Oneonta with excitement over my new life as a college freshman. I had accomplished my goal of escaping the house that I grew up in, now dominated by my mom's alcoholic husband. I had survived my dual life in high school, feeling that I could just be me in this new environment. I pretended to be sad as I hugged my mom, sister Karen, Nan, and Pop good-bye. I was so excited and happy I felt like I would burst.

In those first days of college, I met my best college buddies, registered for my chemistry and calculus classes, and met the most beautiful girl I had ever seen in my life. We walked around and explored our new campus home together with my college roommate, Keith—who I had known since fourth grade.

Even the first college Freshman Chemistry class—when the professor stated to three-hundred students that only three students would be getting an A for the class—was not enough to douse my enthusiasm. As part of the welcome-to-college activities, I fondly remember attending the concert of an up-and-coming rocker, Bruce

Springsteen and the E-Street Band, with nine hundred other SUNY Oneonta students. His first album, *Greetings from Asbury Park NJ*, had two songs that spoke to my soaring spirit, and as a remembrance of my high school years—because I had survived. I had escaped to my new life. By the way, those two songs were *Spirit in the Night* and *Growin' Up*. Those were exciting days.

Hmmm—December 18, 1974: It was my eighteenth birthday, and I was celebrating the last exam of my first semester. I was finally of legal drinking age—although I had been drinking and smoking pot since I was fifteen years old. Especially exciting was that my roommate Keith—whom we all fondly called Doc—and I were two of the only three students that received an A in first semester Chemistry. We were on our way to our chosen fields—Doc was in Pre-Med, and I was in Environmental Engineering. Most excitedly, that beautiful girl I had met on the first day of college was in my room—part of my circle of friends, as we had grown closer over the past few months. Those were exciting and happy days, too.

Hmmm—May 1975: Freshman year was officially over. Doc and I had continued our success in Chemistry, relationships with college buddies were cemented into the next school year, a summer job in the candy department at Grants Department Store was already secured, and that girl—*that girl*—was in my life and had captured my heart. I felt on top of the world at eighteen.

Hmmm—July 1975: The summer was going so well. I worked as many overtime hours as possible at Grants because I was paying my own way through college. The girl had visited my house for a weekend, and it was my turn to meet her parents. I drove a couple hours with huge excitement and anticipation. It was important to make a good impression on her parents. I missed seeing her everyday—her eyes, her smile, her laugh, her playfulness. I arrived to find out she had not taken the day off from her summer lifeguard job—she seemed distant all that day, as I watched her interact with the buff, tanned male lifeguards. My insecurities kicked-in. You know, the same ones that sent me to sit on the log at Wilcox Park four years earlier. I was skinny, not muscular. I had long hair, and it wasn't blonde. I certainly didn't get a nice summer tan working inside at Grants Department Store—although I was proud that I was the youngest department manager in store history.

Maybe living at college was a false world, and those relationships don't extend beyond there. I wasn't sure of anything, except by the time I got home that Sunday night, she had called to say our relationship was over. I was not sure why. My first true love had walked away, and my heart was broken. It would remain that way for a long time.

Hmmm—September 1975: I had such mixed feelings about starting my sophomore year at SUNY Oneonta. I was looking forward to renewing freshman year friendships, registering for Organic

Chemistry with a renewed confidence as one of the top chemistry students at the school, and continuing to hike and explore the Catskill Mountains with my best college buddies when we had free time.

I was hopeful that my first encounter with *her* would be okay—maybe we would be okay back at college and figure things out together. Almost one year from the first moment we met, I ran into her. My heart skipped a beat again. I remembered how much I loved her and how broken my heart was. I still had a glimmer of hope, as we were both in one class together, Introduction to Poetry. In theory, it was my easy class that semester, but it became an emotional roller coaster. I saw her once a week in class, but she barely acknowledged my presence—I thought we could be friends.

It was clear things were over when it was my turn to make a class presentation, and I chose Robert Frost, "The Road Not Taken." She knew I was reciting that poem. As I recall, it was the only Introduction to Poetry class she did not attend that semester. I knew in my head it was over. The rest of that semester I hid my pain well—I was able to balance my classroom success with my fragile emotions by compartmentalizing my life.

When I was not studying Organic Chemistry or Calculus, we were on adventures: climbing the local water tower at night to smoke a joint and gaze at the stars; hiking in the mountains in the snow by the light of a full moon; trying the latest psychedelic while enjoying the Disney classic *Fantasia* on the big screen; playing Frisbee in ten-degree weather until it became so brittle the Frisbee would snap in half; racking up high scores on the pinball machine at one of the many downtown Oneonta bars; running the foosball table all night at The Corner Bar; or driving the eighteen miles to the Unadilla Diner at 1:00 a.m. just because they had the best home-made corn muffins soaked in real butter.

Many times, we would just listen to our favorite rock albums—Emerson, Lake & Palmer, Led Zeppelin, David Bowie, Yes, Pink Floyd, Journey, The Who, Boston, The James Gang, Bachman-Turner Overdrive, Genesis, Grateful Dead, Jethro Tull, Jeff Beck, Lynyrd Skynyrd, and the Allman Brothers—just to name a few of the greats from that era.

There was always an opportunity to party, relax, or create an adventure that would distract my thoughts from her. I was determined that my heartbreak would not impact my studies because it was the first time I had worked to my potential in school—and I wasn't willing to give that up. There were many good times at Littel Hall Third Floor West, but still I wandered campus sometimes hoping to cross her path—just to see her smile for a moment. Maybe talk for a minute. I wasn't expecting answers, just hoping.

Hmmm—December 1975: I managed to get an A in each of my core science and math classes. I received a B in Introduction to Poetry—I guess my mind just wasn't focused while in that class. It was nice to get back home to Red Oaks Mill, if just for a few weeks. I mostly worked the Christmas rush at Grants Department Store, as I always needed the money. Christmas break went fast, and the second semester of my sophomore year began quickly. I felt like I was in a groove, successfully navigating that paper-thin wall that separated my head from my heart.

Hmmm—Sunday, March 14, 1976, 7:00 a.m.: I turned over and put my pillow on my head as the telephone rang early on this Sunday morning. My roommate Doc would answer it, I thought. A moment later, I heard him say, "Dave, it's for you. It's your dad." *Why would my dad be calling on a Sunday—for that matter, he has never called me or visited me at college.*

Doc handed me the telephone. "Hi, Dad. Is everything okay," I asked with concern in my voice. "No, son. I have some bad news," he said, as his voice cracked and quivered trying to get all the words out. He gathered himself and finished, "Your best friend Mike died last night in a car accident." In shock, I responded, "No, that can't be! Are you sure?" "Yes," he said, "It was on the early morning news. He was hit head-on by a drunk driver going the wrong way on Route 9."

I dropped the phone receiver, and as it swung by its cord and hit against our dormitory door, I turned and fell into my bed—sobbing uncontrollably. My best friend—growing up together since that day we met on the banks of Wappinger Creek fourteen years earlier—*was gone.* I don't know how long I cried on my dorm room bed, but when I looked up later, my three best college buddies were sitting in the room—just to be there for me. A few hours later, Doc drove me home to Wappinger Falls so I could attend Mike's funeral service.

As I sat on the swings in Wilbur Park, I now knew the last time I was happy in my life—the day before Mike died. I had emotionally survived my parent's divorce, an alcoholic stepfather, my high school split personality, my freshman year break-up, but after all that there was *not* a lot of emotional stability left in my soul. I crashed and burned after Mike's sudden death.

In those days, there were not a lot of support or therapy groups for young people in trauma. We were supposed to suck it up and go on with our lives—three days of crying, hugging, and a funeral—then back to reality. For me, I felt two of the biggest unexplained losses in my young life in a span of less than a year. That paper-thin wall that had kept my head sane—amid emotional chaos—was now gone. The next twenty months since that day had all been steeply downhill. And here I sat on a swing in Wilbur Park.

I hated that I had given up on my studies and was now failing. I hated that I still missed *her*. I hated that my sisters were impacted even more than I had been from growing up in a dysfunctional family. I hated that I would go to sleep at night just to forget how hungry I was—and then not get up to go to class. I hated my life.

Deep down, I had survivor's guilt. I didn't have the everyday, normal type of survivor's guilt—this was deep-seated survivor's guilt. I had been saved from death by angels, *more than once*—but Mike died, and I wasn't there to prevent it from happening.

My awareness came back to the cold rain as I sat on the swing—and this morning's message of *this is not your life*. I had buried my feelings so deep that the realization I had not been happy since Mike's death created an upwelling of grief, sadness, and desperation—but mostly anger. I jumped off that swing and yelled at the top of my lungs, "WHY God? Why did you take Mike?" I had so much anger I thought I would just burst right then and there. I started pacing back and forth in the rain-soaked grass of Wilbur Park. I yelled, "I am so angry. Why did you save me and not Mike?" I screamed into the grey, cold sky, "I HATE MY LIFE," and began sobbing uncontrollably. I looked down at the wet ground and whispered to myself through my tears, "I hate my life."

I felt so lost and alone. This WAS my life, and I didn't know what to do. I looked up into the sky again and implored from the deepest recesses of my soul, "God, I don't know what to do. I am so lost. This is not my life. Please help me."

At that very moment, a bright light—as bright as the sun—came down through those thick, gray November rain clouds. It came down all the way to Wilbur Park—all the way right to where I was standing. It was a circular shaft of light that surrounded me. I looked down and saw the bright white light touching the ground all around me. I then looked up into the bright shaft of light. It was blinding.

Suddenly, I felt all my anger, my pain, my grief, my depression, my heartbreak—the heaviness of *the life that wasn't mine*—lifting out of my body from my feet all the way through the top of my head. I felt enveloped in love and felt light as a feather—as those heavy emotions left my body. Then I heard a deep male voice in this shaft of healing light, and he said, "Go home." I looked skyward into the light and repeated, "Go home?" I wanted to be sure I heard the message correctly. Once again, he stated, "Go home." And the light was gone as fast as it had appeared. The rain hit my face as it fell from the cold November sky, once again. I fell to my knees. I'm not sure how long I knelt there—in the cold, rain-soaked grass, and mud. Eventually, I went back and sat on the swings to figure out what had just happened.

I'm not even sure how long I sat there on that swing. I was thinking about the events of the morning. It was time to change my life. To get back on the path to what was supposed to be my life—whatever that meant. I thought a lot about going home. That seemed to be an important message, but I didn't really feel like I had a home—was there anything for me in Wappinger Falls?

I came to no immediate conclusions and received no further insights that day. All I knew was that I felt so much better than I had in such a long time. I was no longer angry. I could rationally see that I had been "sleepwalking" through my life—using drugs to avoid the pain—as I dug a deeper and deeper hole of depression. Then and there, I knew I had to change. I got up from that swing, walked back up the hill from Wilbur Park, determined to pick up the pieces of my crumbled life.

I walked in my apartment door intent on taking a hot shower, looking for my textbooks, and going to the campus library to study—trying to remember where the Milne Library was on campus. As I showered, I thought about my grades and how many classes I had missed through the semester. Did I even remember my schedule so I could attend the last classes of the year? And would I even find my textbooks in the apartment? I HAD to find the textbooks—I didn't have enough money to buy them again. Could I even study enough in the next three weeks to recover some of my failing grades? Could I walk into classes that I had not attended since early in the semester? I was not sure of anything—except that an angel came to me this morning to change my life, and God released my pain in the park. I had faith these messages were correct.

In the library that day, I put my plan together to prioritize the classes I thought I had a chance to raise from a failing grade to a C. I needed to at least get a C in each of my chemistry classes: Organic Chemistry III, Analytical Chemistry I, and Physical Chemistry. I decided to take an Incomplete in my physics class—Quantum Mechanics. I also decided not to waste precious study time on my last scheduled final, Differential Equations. That class was hard enough, but I hadn't been to that 8:00 a.m. class in months, and I really hated calculus.

I stayed in Oneonta for Thanksgiving vacation that next week after making an appearance in some classes that I hadn't been to in quite some time. I asked to borrow notes from some students that I recognized. It was difficult, as nothing was online, no classes were recorded, and no study guides were available. If you missed a lecture, you were screwed, and I had missed so many.

After my first three finals, I was happy that I was able to save my grades in my chemistry classes. I only had one more to go—Differential Equations. That night, I finally opened that math textbook to discover the reality—I did not understand a single concept. I would have to walk into that final completely un-prepared. The reality that I was not going to be an engineer had set in—I would eventually change my major to Analytical Chemistry.

On December 16, 1977, I walked across campus to my last final of the semester. The sun was shining. I didn't even notice that it was cold. I felt good inside about what I had accomplished in four short weeks. I felt like I was on the precipice of a new life—a new path.

As I walked through the campus Quad, I noticed a student walking next to me. I glanced at her more closely, and I recognized her from the Introduction to Poetry class I had taken at the beginning of my sophomore year. She was the girl who read that weird Lewis Carol poem, *The Jabberwocky*. I remember clearly, because after the poem was done, I was imploring the Universe, "Please don't let the professor call on me to analyze that poem!" Ms. Capo, the professor, of course called on me to analyze the poem—I was never good with a poker face. All I could think at the time was *why did this girl read such a weird poem?* All I said to the professor was, "I have no idea what that poem was about." I think that secured the B in that class.

Regardless, I now found myself walking right next to the cute Jabberwocky girl a year and a half later. Over the past twenty months, I would not have given it a second thought, and quite honestly, would have avoided the situation altogether. But today was a new day. I said, "Hi. I remember you. You're the Jabberwocky girl." She turned toward me with a look, like what did you just call me! I quickly responded, "We were in the same Introduction to Poetry class about three semesters ago in Phippie Hall." She responded, "And you remembered that I read The Jabberwocky?" I replied, "Yes. It was memorable." I decided not to elaborate.

We had a pleasant walk to our last finals of the semester, which coincidentally were in the same building, same floor, same hallway just two doors down. As we walked into Fitzell Hall together, my heart started pounding and my hands were sweaty as I climbed the stairs to the second floor. I had realized I was about to enter my last and hardest final. I said "good luck on your final" to the Jabberwocky girl and thought that it was a nice distraction, as I entered the classroom I hadn't been in for some time.

At the door, the professor started to hand me the final and realized he didn't recognize me, "This is the Differential Equations final. You must be in the wrong room," he declared with certainty. "I am in the correct room," I replied, and sat down in a chair near the back. I did not recognize any of my classmates who were there to take this final, and from the looks on their faces, they did not recognize me either.

As I scanned the questions on the final exam, it was clear I was going to fail this class. I was hoping the four semesters of calculus I had already successfully completed would help me through this—but I was clearly wrong. I sat there staring at the test for a while and decided I should try to answer a few of the questions, at least. I scribbled nonsensical calculus concepts pretending to answer differential equation final exam questions.

Suddenly, it occurred to me—*why am I doing this*? I was embarrassed to get up and leave so early. *Who cares*, I thought. I don't know these students. They don't know me. They don't know what my life has been like the past twenty months. They don't know an angel came to my bedroom four weeks ago. They don't know I am fixing my life—starting right now. I got up, held my head high, handed in that final exam, and walked out the door. I smiled to myself and thought, *welcome to my new life*.

As fate would have it, the Jabberwocky girl was leaving her final exam at the same time. I was certain she was leaving her final exam early for a much different reason than I was leaving mine.

At that moment, I thought, *we had a pleasant chat on the way— I think I'll catch up to her.* Which is exactly what I did. Three years later, we were married.

A Spiritual Perspective on Prayer

At the time

That Christmas break of my junior year of college, I stayed in Oneonta to work on campus cleaning laboratory glassware for one of the organic chemistry professors. I needed the money to buy food for the upcoming semester, which I decided would be my last. One last semester to try to get my grades back—then I would take off a year to figure out the rest of my life.

I had lots of time to think as I soaped-up, brush-scrubbed, and triple-rinsed every beaker, Erlenmeyer flask, graduated cylinder, and separator flask in all the labs for $7.50 per hour. I was happy. Happy to know this *was* my life—back on track. Thankful that an angel woke me up that cold rainy morning.

And thankful that God had answered my prayers in the park—a prayer that resonated deep, deep within my soul. And thankful I had saved a few of my grades. And grateful that I finally had a future to look forward to—whatever that might be. It didn't matter, really, because I knew I had benevolent forces by my side. As the song *Amazing Grace* goes, "*I once was lost but now am found.*"

As I write today

At its core, prayer is a soul-level communication that travels at the speed of light into the Universe. The structure of a prayer must be constructed as a viable message with clear intent as it travels as a light wave through a sea of electromagnetic energy, with its unique frequency and intended destination.

Words matter. Words have literal meanings. You don't want your prayer to be misconstrued. The words *want*, *need*, or *desire* are commonly used words when people construct prayer requests. Let's take a closer glimpse of the dual nature of those words from the Merriam-Webster dictionary:

Definition of *want:*

As an intransitive verb:	*to be needy or destitute*
As a transitive verb:	*to suffer from the lack of*
As a noun	*lack, deficiency*

Definition of *need*

As an intransitive verb:	*to be in want*
As a transitive verb:	*require*
As a noun	*lack of subsistence; poverty*

Definition of *desire*

As an intransitive verb:	*to have or feel desire*
As a transitive verb:	*to hope for*
As a noun	*longing, craving*

When using these words in the construction of a prayer, your prayer could be answered literally—as you continue to *be needy, destitute, suffer from lack of, to be in want of, to continue to hope for and crave*—for your specific prayer request outcome.

This type of prayer reinforces your request to continue without! And it becomes a self-fulfilling prophecy that God does not answer prayers, when in fact, you received *exactly* what you prayed for.

As an alternative, prayer can be your message of gratitude. Gratitude for the gifts God has given you. And gratitude for the gifts God is manifesting into your life—*but have not yet arrived in your physical time-space dimension*. It is a thank you for what you know will be literally ahead for your highest good. It is a message of gratitude for the awesome ability to co-create our individual realities in partnership with the Universal energy of God.

Finding Clarity:
> *Am I able to pray from the deepest recesses of my heart*
> *and soul to ask for—and be grateful for—help and guidance?*

Remember, the Universe is not constrained by time or space, so a heartfelt thank you prayer of gratitude can manifest results immediately or may take a bit of time. Be appreciative of the complex amount of life-changing maneuvering your prayer request might require. Be patient.

Many times, I have said a prayer of gratitude after a prior prayer had *not* been answered. I understand now it must have been for my highest good. Or maybe, if granted, it would have shifted my life's path to a destination that was not part of my herebefore soul plan. Since our free will can override a herebefore soul plan, I have gotten into the habit of ending all prayers with the phrase, "... *if this is for my highest good. Amen.*" This phrase specifically realigns your prayer request with your own soul's herebefore plan—the reason you chose to come here to Earth at this time.

Words have meaning. Decide today to use prayers of gratitude. Initiate an abundance mindset. Initiate prayer from your deepest core—your heart and soul. Be thankful for all blessings already received. And those blessings in the queue on their way to be manifested into your present reality. Live in gratitude. Every day.

Daily Affirmation

I am grateful for all the blessings in my life,
even those blessings that are yet to arrive in the present.

"The eyes see only what the mind is prepared to comprehend."

~**Henri Bergson, French Philosopher**

Chapter Nine

The Train to Susquehanna

A Spiritual Perspective on Perception

That Old Teddy Bear

David K. Munson ©2023

*Hold on tight and don't let go
of the hurt you feel,
and the pain you know.*

*Hug it like an old teddy bear
while it bleeds your soul,
not knowing you are unaware.*

*So just reach in and cut the cord
and release negative patterns
to which you are moored.*

*Realize it all was created by you.
So, forgive yourself and live renewed,
as many life options are in the queue.*

The phone was ringing and, although I did not feel like talking to anyone, I answered it anyway. It was a familiar voice on the other end, Twig, one of my freshman year roommates who had moved off campus. We called him Twig because he was so skinny, although he had a big personality. "Dave, I am so sorry to hear about your hometown friend dying. If there's anything I can do to help, or you just want to talk, or if you just need to get away, just call me anytime," he said. Half-heartedly, I replied, "Thanks Twig." He ignored my indifference and continued, "This Sunday is going to be nice and sunny. How about we jump a train and go for a ride?"

Twig and I used to talk about jumping a train in the Oneonta rail yard and just traveling to wherever it took us. At the time, anyone within earshot of our conversation thought we were nuts, but we both had adventurous spirits. He continued, "I'll pack lunch, you don't need to bring anything. Meet me at my house at dawn on Sunday. This will be fun." I knew he was really trying to get my mind off the pain of Mike's death. I said, "Sure, let's do it."

Sunday morning arrived and the weather was beautiful, as Twig predicted. This was a rarity in Oneonta, NY, in the spring. As I walked off campus, down the cow path hill toward town, I was thankful for the good weather but apprehensive on how we could safely jump a train. I wondered whether there would even be a Delaware and Hudson train leaving the Oneonta rail yard that morning. For all I knew, we could be arrested for trespassing, or worse. A part of me was hoping there was no train, and we would just go to breakfast at the downtown diner.

When I arrived at Twig's house, he was already sitting on the steps ready to go. As we left, his girlfriend Jo implored us to be careful. "We'll be careful," I said as we walked away down the sidewalk, "and we'll either see you in an hour or around dinner time." Jo yelled back, "If you're back in an hour, I'll make you a big break-fast of bacon and eggs!" I could tell that's what she was hoping. But she followed it up with, "If you're later, I'll have dinner ready!"

Our walk toward the rail yard was filled with excitement, anticipation, and strategy. Which direction should we ride, northbound or southbound? Should we jump a boxcar closer to the train engine or closer to the caboose? What is the best way to jump into the train if it's moving? So many questions for novice vagabonds. The one thing we knew for sure is we would look for a boxcar where the doors were open on both sides, so we could fully enjoy the scenery and this beautiful Upstate New York sunny day.

There were no other people in sight on this early Sunday morning. Everyone was still asleep from a Saturday night of partying in this college town. I thought that was good, as we would not be seen trying to sneak into the rail yard where dozens of trains moved along the Delaware and Hudson tracks every day carrying cargo through the southern tier of New York State to other destinations.

Our first challenge was quite easy, as there was a hole in the rusty chain-link fence along the perimeter of the rail yard—no challenge for two skinny college kids. We squatted down behind some bushes to check out the situation. Fortunately, we did not see any rail yard workers, but there were very few trains on this Sunday morning. Suddenly, as if on cue, a train whistle blew, and we saw the exhaust billowing up from an engine about a hundred yards away. That was a good sign, as one of the few trains at the site began to move. "I guess we're heading south," Twig exclaimed. I was glad because I really didn't want to end up in Canada!

We ran as fast as we could over the dozen or so empty tracks and spotted the perfect boxcar with doors open on both sides. As we approached that red boxcar, it was clear the train was going faster than we had expected. And was picking up steam! We were surprised how high the floor of the boxcar was—*could we even make the jump safely*, I thought. As I always do in these situations, I said a prayer to my guardian angels to protect us, and I listened carefully for any warning of impending danger. I was unsure if I could hear a warning. The metal-on-metal screeching of the train wheels on the tracks was very loud as we ran alongside this moving train. Suffice it to say we jumped into the train safely—I boosted Twig into the moving boxcar, and he pulled me up—just in the nick of time as the boxcar passed by the rail yard master's station. We were on our way!

Now that the dangerous part of our adventure was behind us, or so we thought, I was completely relaxed and was enjoying our ride—being present in the moment. As we sat at the edge of the boxcar dangling our legs out the door, we could hear the engine's whistle as it passed through train crossings. That sound comforted me. I felt safe. We saw beautiful, peaceful Upstate New York farms, cows in the pastures, morning dew glistening off the trees, the smell of freshly plowed fields ready for the spring sowing. The scenery was breathtaking as the train glided over hill and dale. We also saw people along the way—mostly sitting in their cars waiting patiently at railroad crossings. Many were all dressed up for church —they would point, smile, and wave. We would smile and wave back, as our long hair blew in the wind created by the speed of the train racing down the rails to our unknown destination.

I think everyone has a fantasy of hopping the rails and traveling throughout this beautiful country. Even if for a little while, Twig and I were doing just that. Occasionally, I would observe some teenagers on bikes along the tracks watching the train go by. It reminded me of when Mike and I would spend sunny summer days lying on the railroad tracks near Maloney Road while Led Zeppelin's *Houses of the Holy* blasted on his portable D-battery-powered eight-track tape player. I was happy to remember this good memory while still living in the shadow of his death, and I was so appreciative of Twig's idea to go on this journey.

Earlier that morning, we had discussed our plan of how to get off the train. Obviously, we weren't going to jump out of a moving train. We assumed it would be stopping, or at a minimum, slowing down, in the biggest city south of Oneonta—Binghamton, NY. We would get off there, giving us an easy opportunity to hitchhike north on I-88 and back to Oneonta just in time for Jo's dinner. These days, we could have used our cell phone GPS to tell us exactly where we were, but back then we just had to guess and hope the plan worked out.

At some point during our trip, the train began to slow down. We assumed it was approaching the Binghamton, NY, rail yard. As the train slowed, we were ready to jump out of the boxcar, so we weren't spotted by the authorities. We were prepared to run as fast as we could to evade capture. None of that happened. The train came to a complete stop and all we could see on all sides was dense forest. Did they stop because they had discovered us?

We jumped down and decided to walk to the front of the train to ask why it had stopped—or some similar question. We passed more than forty boxcars as we walked toward the train's engine. The train conductor was very nice in explaining why we had stopped due to train traffic, etc. and the train would be on its way in an hour or so.

Twig and I decided to walk back to the last rail crossing where there would be a road. We could maybe figure out where we were and how to get home. Luckily, there were kids playing baseball in the street, so we approached them and asked, "Where are we?" They looked at us strangely, and asked, "Are you hippies?" I replied with a smile, "No, we were on the train. It broke down and we need to find a pay phone. So, where are we?" The bigger kid replied, "Maple Street." I continued, "What city?" In unison, they said, "Susquehanna." Surprised, I replied, "Susquehanna, Pennsylvania!" They said, "Yup," and they returned to tossing the baseball back and forth.

"Which way to town?" Twig inquired. One of them pointed and said, "That-a-way." So, we turned and started walking that-a-way! We had traveled much further south than our original plan—more than sixty miles south from where we started the day.

Eventually, we were quite relieved to see a sign to I-81 North, but our relief was stifled by the approaching dark storm clouds coming in from the west. We stood at the entrance ramp to I-81 North—somewhere near Susquehanna, Pennsylvania—for an hour as the thunder, lightning, and rain clouds approached. Car after car passed us by—two long-haired college kids hitchhiking.

The rain arrived, more like a downpour. We were not prepared for rain. We had left earlier in the day in sunshine and clear blue skies. Now we were completely drenched in another state, far away from home, with no money or food. We tucked our wet hair into the back collar of our shirts and stuck out our thumbs praying for a ride. We were hoping to change the perception of drivers passing us by. And it worked because a car stopped—and to our surprise, it was an older couple who felt sorry for us standing out in a rainstorm. We thanked them profusely and appreciated that they had turned up the heat in the car as we headed north back toward Oneonta. Unfortunately, they were only able to drive us a short distance. That would be the last normal ride Twig and I would have the rest of the day.

It seemed like hours we stuck our thumbs into the air each time a car drove up the entrance ramp to the interstate. We decided to change plans and walked to one of the local, two-lane country roads heading north hoping to change our luck. And it worked!

Soon enough a big red pickup truck whizzed by, put on its brakes, and backed up to see if we needed a ride and where we were going. Twig and I were thrilled to be moving north in the back seat of a half-cab truck—only one set of doors on each side. The three guys in the front—all donning cowboy hats, short hair, and Pabst Blue Ribbons—seemed friendly enough, as we described our experience riding the rails. Our perception was that the conversation was going well, and we were safe. Then I heard them whispering to each other "*those hippie freaks back there.*" Immediately, I received a message from Nathaniel, "David, get out of there. You are in danger."

Unlike other times in my life, I didn't have to ask "What?" I felt the danger. I leaned toward Twig, who was sitting to my right and directly behind the passenger seat, and said, "We are in danger. We must bail out at our first opportunity." He must have felt it, too, because he didn't even question when I pointed to the front seat release button near the floor, motioned that when he released it,

I would push the passenger seat forward, while he lunged to grab the door handle, open the door, and we would jump out.

It seemed like an impossible task, as we were trapped in the backseat of this pickup truck traveling at fifty-five miles per hour down a country highway. All I knew was those guys were big, drunk, and now were very vocal about us hippie college boys. But I also knew we had angels on our side.

The next few minutes seemed like an eternity as we waited for our opportunity to attempt our escape. I was praying for a stoplight, but nothing was there except more country road, thick dense forest, deer crossing signs, cow pastures, and the occasional dirt side road. Suddenly, we heard one of them say, "Let's turn here," as he pointed to the left. That was our chance, and I heard Nathaniel say to me, "Now!"

As the truck slowed and started to turn left, it was perfect. Twig released the front seat; I slammed it forward so hard one of the guys hit their head on the front windshield as the truck was mid-turn. Twig reached forward and grabbed the door handle releasing the front passenger door—in perfect concert with the centrifugal force of the turn—and it swung wide open. I was right behind Twig as he didn't hesitate to jump out onto the concrete road. We rolled into the middle of the highway, just as the red pickup truck turned off onto a narrow, dirt back road. Dust was flying off their tires as they attempted a messy three-point turn in the dirt.

Twig and I did not wait around. We jumped up and ran into the dense forest as fast as we could. We felt like we had evened the odds, as two skinny hippie college boys could probably outrun three drunk mad cowboys in the woods of the southern tier of New York State. As we hunkered down about fifty yards off the highway, we saw the red pickup truck drive back-and-forth down this stretch of road for nearly an hour. For quite a while, we hiked north in the woods, parallel to the highway toward the safety of home. We were not thinking about the cuts and bruises from rolling on the highway—we knew it would have been much, much worse had we not escaped.

Our thoughts turned to Jo back home, who was probably very worried, as we were way past due for the dinner she had promised. But we had no way to contact her. So, when the darkness of the day finally descended, we felt kind of safe, as we hadn't seen the red pickup for a while. We hiked back to the highway to hitchhike in the dark. It seemed like an eternity as headlights whizzed by us every few minutes. As they passed us by, we just turned and took another step north.

Finally, a set of headlights started slowing down. Our first thought was to ensure it wasn't the red truck—and it wasn't. It was a rusty, old white cargo van, the kind with no windows in the back. Twig and I were very suspicious. We had another perception—that getting in this white van was not a good idea. So, we stood outside the passenger window and asked a few questions—like where were they going, why did they stop, did they mind our long hair? Could we get an idea of what their perception was of us? It was especially helpful they were traveling to the dirt bike races near Oneonta, and Twig knew about dirt bikes and motorcycles. On my part, I just listened—not to their answers, but for a warning of any sort that might indicate we should run back into the dense woods for protection. We decided to accept their offer of a north-bound ride.

They opened the back doors to reveal a few more guys in the back sitting around an active beer keg. *Oh boy, here we go*, I thought. Twig insisted we sit right behind the keg next to the back doors. I knew exactly what he was thinking . . . so we could escape.

And the conversation about motorcycles continued while we reluctantly accepted a fresh pour into the shiny red Solo cups. I prayed the driver was not too drunk to drive. I prayed for us to get home safely. I listened for Nathaniel's warning.

These guys—on their way to the dirt bike races—were interested in college town activities. So naturally, the conversation turned to our college, SUNY Oneonta, and the high density of bars bustling with female college students. We had them hooked—college town, college girls, bars. We negotiated a deal for them to drive *past* their original destination all the way to Oneonta. In exchange, we would show them where all the good bars were located. At the end of the day, I was relieved we weren't lying in some back road field bloodied and beaten. Our odd barter had worked out. Forty-five minutes later they dropped us off in Twig's driveway. Jo was waiting at the door. I had wished there was someone like her waiting for me somewhere. I was grateful for Twig. I was grateful for Nathaniel in my life.

A Spiritual Perspective on Perception

At the time

I did wonder how we jumped from that moving truck without breaking our bodies, much less getting away with only a few scratches and bruises. Did an army of angels cushion our fall? How did we end up in a van full of drunk guys who were nice enough to drive us all the way home? So many questions without answers. The day was full of emotions, to be sure.

The day also was filled with incorrect perceptions of reality. We perceived it would be easy to jump a train. We perceived the sun would be shining all day. We perceived we were still in New York, when we had traveled all the way into Pennsylvania. We perceived old people wouldn't pick up long-haired hippie hitchhikers. We perceived young guys in a pickup truck were safe, and guys in a rusty cargo van were not. My perspective was as a young, naïve, teenage college student. My perceptions were fleeting.

As I write today

The accumulation of your life experiences, emotional growth, and spiritual growth creates the basis for your perspective—*your point of view*—toward any event or circumstance at any moment in time. Your intellectual thoughts, observations, and/or interpretation about a specific moment in time or event is your *perception.* A metaphor:

Two Buddhist monks were sitting together on top of a mountain peak in the Himalayas. One was adorned with the most colorful burgundy red robe that complemented his long, gray beard. His years of wisdom were mapped on his wrinkled face, but his eyes twinkled as if he was still in the dawn of his life.

The other monk was obviously new to the Buddhist monastery, as he was still adorned in the dull brown robe issued upon his arrival a few months ago. The silence was broken by his inquiry, "Master teacher, why are we here on this mountaintop?" The calm response was, "Shhhhh." After quite some time, the master teacher opened his eyes and spoke, "Young lad, do you think we have the same perspective?" The young monk contemplated his answer and finally replied, "Yes. Both of us are here sitting on this mountaintop. That is our perspective." The master teacher smiled and spoke, "Yes, young one. You answer in the literal sense. We are both on this mountaintop. But I am an old monk sitting on this mountaintop, and you are a young monk sitting on this mountaintop. We have different perspectives." The young monk nodded affirmingly, "I understand."

The master teacher saw this as a teaching moment, so he continued this dialogue, "Do you understand fully? Tell me what you perceive as we sit here from this perspective." The young monk's eyes widened, as he knew this must be an important question. He scanned the horizon. He scanned the valley below.

He even studied the rocky crags just below their resting spot before replying, "I see white clouds gently floating in an azure sky. I see a blue whistling thrush flitting among the alder trees. I see glistening peaks of pure white snow beckoning us to play. I see the whitecaps of a restless stream rapidly traveling through the valley below. And to top that off, I see the ant struggling to climb over that piece of granite—the granite that makes this mountain so sturdy." The young monk held his head up high, proud of his response.

"Yes, once again, your perceptions are quite literal and your descriptions beautifully spoken," came the reply from his master teacher. Boldly, the young monk decided to ask, "Master teacher, what do you perceive?" The young monk was taken aback as his teacher closed his eyes for what seemed like minutes. Finally, the moment came for the master teacher to speak. The young monk leaned forward in anticipation of a potential answer even more descriptive than his. "I perceive God," came the simple reply.

Perspective is truly a personal thing. Even though facts are facts, people look at them through different life-altered lenses—their personal perspective. The interpretation of facts is processed through our individual filters leading each of us to potentially similar, different, or unique perceptions of the exact same reality.

Personal and/or spiritual growth changes how we look at things—our perspective—thereby modifying our perceptions. In other words, even though the facts of my experiences recounted in this book remain burned into my memory, my perceptions of these experiences have evolved over time.

I can just imagine there are many ways to perceive the adventure Twig and I had on our train to Susquehanna that spring day in 1976—depending upon your perspective. Some might say we were foolish—even acting in a dangerous way—to jump a train. Some may say we were lucky. Some might say it was stupid to jump out of a moving truck onto the concrete road, just because I *might have* heard a warning voice. Some might say we took advantage of a group of horny, drunk guys. Some might say we were wrong to make Jo worry well into the night. Some might say Twig was a great friend to initiate this adventure to get my mind off Mike's death—even if only for a day. The truth is: *each of those perceptions appear correct from different perspectives.* What didn't change was that those events happened. Perspective changes perceptions.

We come to this existence to experience life. Some souls may want to experience forgiveness. Some souls may want to experience overcoming abuse. Some souls may want to experience helping animals. Some souls may want to experience unconditional love. Some souls may want to experience overcoming poverty. Some souls may want to experience physical challenges. Some souls may want to experience working with the earth. Some souls may want to experience being charitable. Some souls may want to experience co-creating with God. Some souls come just to be with and support the souls they have been with in previous lives. Some souls want to experience it all.

The life challenges we desire to experience in a physical existence are sometimes too much to overcome, and we get lost in the chaos of this time-space existence. I've been there. We forget to reach out to our guardian angels, spirit guides, and to God. Sometimes we even blame God. Sometimes damaged souls even check out of this life.

Sometimes souls get stuck in one type of situation repeatedly. The situations that keep showing up in *your life* are the most defining clues to what you planned before you came to Earth. In the Herebefore, you had great intent to experience certain things in this dimension. Of course, you have free will to continue with the experiences you pre-planned. Or you can choose differently to alter what you had once desired in the herebefore. Allow me another metaphor (*aren't metaphors fun*):

> *Let's visualize our spiritual growth as a journey up a mountain. Not straight up but circling around and around the mountain on a continuous spiral path upward. On this journey, there are stopping areas where you could stay and experience life—we'll call them life-experience areas. These life-experience areas*

show up along your personal journey—because you chose them in the herebefore.

And of course, you pull into those areas, even though you read the sign, "Life-Experience Area—Dysfunctional Relationship Ahead— Learn Self-Confidence." Because that's what you chose to experience—to grow spiritually. Some will get stuck right there, and there they will stay in that dysfunctional relationship.

For many, there comes a crisis point, or an awakening, that motivates them to change their life. Some people may just want to escape, so up the mountain they go—learning and growing. They journey around and around to a higher portion of the mountain until they get to the side of the mountain where the view looks similar—kind of like where they just left. It feels like a comfortable place to stop on their life journey. They might even think that this one's different because they've grown— emotionally and spiritually—and now have a different perspective. And the Universe asks, "Have you really grown?"

And they miss the next sign, "Life-Experience Area 1 mile— Emotional Abuse Ahead—Learn Forgiveness." So, they pull into that next stopping area—that next life experience. And so on and so on . . . until the day they finally see the light and drive right past that sign in their spiritual growth journey up the mountain.

And the Universe knows, "You have grown." You have learned self-confidence and forgiveness—no need to pull into that life-experience area ever again. The Universe will always present you with growth and learning opportunities—more life-experience areas, so to speak.

You have free will to choose. Choose to experience the life that serves your highest good—your spiritual growth. And if you are stuck in a life-experience area, simply restart your spiritual journey up the mountain. Read the signs. Make choices from an awakened soul, aware that the Universe is giving you an opportunity for spiritual growth. Or reply to the Universe, "I see the sign, and I choose to continue my spiritual journey without a repeat of that lesson." Your guardian angels will be with you. God will be with you. They will smile.

This might be the hardest lesson ever—to overcome our egos and take responsibility for the experiences that show up in our lives. We can choose to play the victim, choose to continue to allow abuse, continue to stew in anger over being mistreated, continue addiction, or we can choose to change our life, change our mind, heal, forgive, reach out to each other, reach out to God. Find the silver lining. Find the joy in your journey.

I am confident that as you read this book, you will have a unique experience, a unique perception of the information presented based upon your personal perspective. And that's okay. And if you read it again ten years from now, your perceptions may be different—maybe from a higher perspective as you journey up your own mountain.

Finding Clarity:
Am I able to see that the situations that continue to show up in my life are the lessons I have chosen to experience?

Let's look at the perspectives and perceptions that impact most people—*your family*. Have you ever had a conversation with your siblings about their experience growing up in your own family? As you might suspect, there would be many commonalities in how you all perceived the experience. What may surprise you is that there also would be many differences. Each sibling having a different perspective, resulting in different perceptions of growing up in the same family.

In my life, my younger sister, Karen, and I had a much different perceptions of growing up in the same house. I didn't realize it until I was twenty years old. Karen and I were sitting in her almost-brand-new brown Chevy Camaro. It was parked in the grass of the front yard of the house we grew up in. She was hoping someone speeding past 329 New Hackensack Road would see the newly placed for sale sign in its window, stop, and buy her car. At the age of nineteen, she needed the money to move to California. I wondered why she was moving so far away. As we sat there, she finally began to explain why she was "*running away from her life.*"

She revealed to me that our dad had been sexually abusing her since she was ten years old. I was shocked to hear those words. I was so angry and confused, but certainly nothing compared to the anger and confusion she had endured during her formative years. I don't have to go into detail about how different our individual perceptions of growing up in our family were. My dad—hard worker, fun guy, and baseball coach. Her dad—sexual abuser. Same dad. Same family. Completely different experiences. Completely different life-altering perspectives.

It is valuable to point out a conversation that Karen and I had many years later. In 2002, my sisters and I traveled to Ft. Lauderdale, Florida from different parts of the United States because our dad had died. We already knew his third wife had cremated his remains days earlier and there was to be no formal funeral or ceremony. We just wanted to be together on the beach in Florida—maybe to remember the good times camping or playing baseball—or maybe for some unloading of painful memories and cathartic healing. I was prepared for both, as I was the only one who had seen him in many years. I was able to tell them that Dad had also suffered childhood trauma from an emotionally abusive alcoholic mother, and that even her father was an alcoholic who had created an unsafe home environment, too. Who knows how far back our family's generational cycle of abuse went. What we did acknowledge to each other on that beach was that we would stop that cycle here and now—into the next generation with our own children.

At one point Karen shared, "I always wanted to be a chiropractor, but because of the abuse, I was not a good student, so Dad took that away from me." Giving her my perspective on that statement was one of the most difficult things I've ever had to do, as I replied:

"Your journey in this life was agreed upon before you arrived on this Earth. The sexual abuse moved your life to a pre-destined path of helping other children who have also experienced childhood trauma—especially on the Ojibwa Reservation in Northern Wisconsin. You have served on national committees advocating for abused children, you have resurrected a Boys and Girls Club, provided a haven for those kids, and started a school program for misunderstood truant high school girls called Mastering the Journey. From my perspective, all your accomplishments dwarf how you could have helped as a chiropractor. Your higher-self decided to come to this Earth—chose these parents—to experience childhood trauma for the soul purpose to heal many, many other traumatized kids and change their lives. A master healer's journey."

After I made my point, there was silence. I was praying she would not be upset or mad at me for voicing what I felt was a higher truth—*a different perspective*. After what seemed like a long while, she nodded and said something like, "I can understand that." Nearly twenty years later, she documented her lifetime of healing, and helping others through their own healing journeys, in her book, *Just A Girl – Our Challenge to Heal Childhood Trauma*, by Karen Ann Harden. If you are so moved, purchase a copy, and read her story about personal healing through connecting with others who have experienced childhood trauma and need to be in a healing space, too.

Manipulated Perceptions

The information presented in this section is merely intended to help you look at our world from another angle—from a different perspective. Maybe to just take one small step toward dissolving the perceived boundaries that artificially separate us. Although we all have our individual journeys here on Earth, we are rapidly approaching a *collective branching* on humanity's tree of life—toward a world of only-love. It is time to awaken each other, to nudge our collective consciousness toward that goal.

Unfortunately, humanity is being led down another path where darkness will eventually divide, conquer, and control human souls through manipulated perceptions. Or at a minimum, disconnect us from each other while we are distracted or are engrossed in the latest "crisis" perceptions.

It does not have to be this way. Collectively, we can manifest a path onto the branch where all human souls live in only-love with no separation. We just must change our perspective. To see it for what it is—a manipulation of our attention away from both our spirituality and our God-given gifts of individuality within the Oneness.

In our world today, perspectives, perceptions, and how we filter individually is impacted not only by our personal experiences but by a larger collective group narrative. This marketing phenomenon—this manipulated perception—is called *groupthink*.

History is filled with rich examples of when groupthink was used as an effective weapon—a fear-based control tactic. I will relay a parable, based upon historical events, about human souls who were misled with a manipulated perception and awakened too late:

> *Six years before the start of World War II, the National Socialist Party in Germany had solidified its power under an aging and feeble president. The German economy had undergone many years of economic turmoil after World War I, and a depression had already started halfway around the world in the United States. Those in power took the opportunity manipulate perceptions by placing blame on scapegoats—the Jewish population in Europe. By 1938, vast networks of detention camps, where their political opponents, undesirables, and persons determined by the Third Reich as exhibiting asocial behavior, had already been arrested and detained without any due process through a corrupted judicial system. By the end of 1941, the German minister of transportation had already*

coordinated resettlement trains throughout Europe—a euphemism for transporting Jews to extermination death camps. Meanwhile, the countries of the western civilizations, including the United States, chose to placate the bully for many years and turned a blind eye to the genocide being perpetrated at the hands of the German National Socialist Party within their so-called resettlement camps. It is very possible the scene described below at the Warsaw Central Railway Station in Poland, circa 1943, may have occurred, or something very similar:

Three rabbis stood along the train platform separated by some distance, as the boxcars were lined up as far as one could see. A reporter from the local newspaper was there to report on the progress. Thousands of men, women, and children were lined up ready to board the train's boxcars for relocation. They wore their best clothes with the forced Jewish badge—a yellow star— carefully sewn onto their shirts or coats. Many were carrying one small suitcase with some clothes along with a few precious family heirlooms and photographs. Many just held the hands of their young children or spent time propping up their elderly parent in the heat. One rabbi was walking through the lines reassuring his flock with a smile and kind words. He perceived that resettlement by the National Socialist Party was a great idea and would result in a better life than living in the Warsaw ghetto.

Meanwhile, down the train platform was a second rabbi. He was standing near the doors of an old boxcar with peeling, red paint. Sweat rolled down his face from under his yarmulke. He tried to hide the concern for his flock, but his eyes were a revealing window into his tortured soul. He had his suspicions about where this train was going and tried to put the thought out of his mind. He remained stoic as the SS Police were nearby, and they had guns. None of the Jews had owned guns since 1939, as the German government enacted laws prohibiting enemies of the National Socialist state, including all Jewish persons, from possessing any dangerous weapons, including firearms. His flock was only armed with the hope of a brighter future. And there he stood, obediently.

Suddenly, a commotion broke out at the far end of the loading platform. A third rabbi was shouting to the families in line, "Run away! Try to escape! They are not sending you for relocation. They are sending you to your death at an extermination camp!" The Jews in line looked at him with confusion. How could that be, they thought. Human beings couldn't possibly do that to each other! Within moments, an SS guard came over and knocked the rabbi unconscious with the butt of his Karabiner 98k Mauser. The SS guard turned toward the Jews and said, "Nothing to see here people. Just a troublemaker conspiracy theorist. You should be more concerned with the storm clouds overhead.

Now hurry up and move along into that boxcar." The next morning, the New Courier of Warsaw newspaper published the headline, *"Local Rabbi Pleased as a Few Hundred Families Leave for Resettlement."* Not a word of this event was mentioned in the other two Warsaw newspapers.

The free will of those souls already standing in line at the train station had already been wrested away. Groupthink prevailed in the hands of darkness. Manipulated perceptions lulled an unsuspecting, innocent population into a brutal period of man's inhumanity to man.

Historically, some people were awake. They were able to recognize the gradual implementation of tyranny and implemented their free will before it was too late. Some people used their free will to warn others. Some people used their free will to escape with their families. Some people used their free will to form underground resistance groups. Some people used their free will to save others.

Who do you relate to in the above metaphor? Are you the Jewish adult in line marked with a yellow star; or are you the naïve rabbi with rose-colored glasses; or are you the aware rabbi suffering in silence; or the brave whistleblower rabbi verbalizing the truth. Maybe unwittingly, you are the obedient German guard controlling the process as part of your job. Maybe consciously, you are the newspaper reporter reinforcing the groupthink narrative on behalf of the power structure to manipulate an unsuspecting population. Even worse, the editors of the other newspapers who decided to bury the story, justifying their actions to keep their status in the prevailing power structure. They all played a role in history. Unfortunately, all these roles play out in our world today. Similar roles. Slightly different groupthink narrative.

In America, manipulation of our perceptions was probably going on way before the present time, but in 2012 the pace quickened because manipulating information, suppressing the news, and obscuring the truth in the media became *legal:*

> *On December 29, 2012, HR 4310 was signed. The 2013 National Defense Authorization Act. Section 1078 of the bill authorized the use of propaganda inside the United States, which was banned since 1948.*

Like me, you may have thought propaganda was only used in totalitarian governments and communist countries. That is why a discussion of this groupthink concept is necessary in a spiritual book. Because we are in a spiritual battle right now that is being manipulated through the control, modification and/or suppression of information in America. And even more concerning, during this time, a handful of people and companies bought up and merged control of *all media worldwide.*

As Barbara Marciniak, author and channeler, states, "The ultimate tyranny in a society is not control by martial law. It is control by the psychological manipulation of consciousness, through which reality is defined so that those that exist within it do not even realize that they are in prison. They do not even realize that there is something outside of where they exist."

I must ask a tough question, something you may not want to consider. Who will be the modern-day scapegoats? Whose souls will be targeted as being dangerous through manipulated perceptions? Whose souls will be condemned because they are not complying with a controlled narrative filled with not-love?

The simplest way to interpret any human interaction or group dynamic is to ask yourself: *Does this situation reflect love or fear—the freedom to choose love or be manipulated by fear?* Fear creates soul blindness.

It's right in front of us—and hard to look at. I am so sorry that I must point out the messiness in our world that is separating God's children. My intention is not to create fear. It is to awaken us. Because it's easy to forget that each one of us is a child of God. Because it's too easy to become complacent.

We must set-aside our fear and move forward together with love and common sense—to utilize our own personal information filters developed through a lifetime of experiences. We need to be awake or God-loving people will be next onto those historical "relocation camp" trains. I tell you this, those trains do not exist in the only-love world that our collective consciousness journey can create.

Each one of us must decide what information we internalize that either narrows, broadens, or completely alters our perspective—the angle at which we look at things. That angle of perspective changes our interpretation of past, present, or future events with maybe even a nugget of healing. With maybe even the motivation to take us one step toward our awakening.

So, let's change the narrative. Don't be silenced within a manipulated narrative of fear and control. Let's rise above it. You will be surprised how many people are waking up, looking around with a new perspective, and shining their light to dispel darkness.

Acts of love bring people together, connecting us without repercussion or judgment, and allowing each of us the safety to exist with our own beliefs, without fear. The vastness of love within us is much greater than we even imagine. We are powerful when we are together. And the only thing darkness is afraid of is our awakening.

Daily Affirmation

I entrust my higher self to expand my perspective, question my perceptions, and fulfill my soul's destiny.

"I regret not death. I am going to meet my friends in another world."

~Ludovico Ariosto, 15th Century Italian Poet

Chapter Ten

A Glimpse of the Hereafter

A Spiritual Perspective on Death

Between the Herebefore

David K. Munson ©2021

*Living our lives in a physical space
between the herebefore and the hereafter.
Without our conscious awareness,
the veil conceals an unwrapped gift.*

*Living our lives in a time race
between the herebefore and the hereafter.
Earthly abundance ebbs and flows,
and through the rubble we each sift.*

*Living our lives in an empty embrace
between the herebefore and the hereafter.
We hold tight to the ego's illusion,
and from our true selves we each drift.*

*Living our lives with extraordinary grace
between the herebefore and the hereafter.
Our hearts reconnect with all that is One,
creating a healing of our rift.*

Along my journey, I have been blessed to receive glimpses of the hereafter from loved ones. Growing up with an understanding that there was more to this life than I could comprehend helped me to be open. Open to receiving signs and messages from the other side of the veil. I am certain that I have missed many signs and messages, too.

The experiences others have shared with me, along with situations I have personally experienced—a few of them in this book—have led me to a strong belief. We exist in our space-time dimension surrounded by energies and entities that are just on the other side of the veil. We are connected by vibrational frequencies and disconnected only by our perceptions.

Here I share three stories of relatives and my experiences surrounding their transition to the next existence. In our world, we call this death. Like all of life's unique moments, each of these stories is personal for the people involved. I hope I have honored them by properly sharing their transition stories with you.

<u>Kenneth</u>: *The Garden Gate*

Earlier in these writings, I told of my paternal grandfather Pop M, a devout atheist for much of his life—until *the garden gate*. The Munson family history is rife with men who died young of heart attacks, except about six generations ago. Oddly enough, one of my distant relatives died in his early thirties from a kick to the head as he drove mules to pull barges on the Erie Canal.

Nonetheless, Pop was in good shape, as he always had physical jobs—milkman, bread delivery, etc. But that did not prevent him from avoiding the family history of heart attacks. His dad, a Hudson River dock worker in Poughkeepsie, NY, died in his mid-forties. The difference was that Pop survived his first heart attack.

While still in the hospital, he recounted his experience to his oldest son—my dad. You see, my grandfather had died from that first heart attack and came back—an atheist with a strong belief that there was nothing after this life except the deep-six—a term used to describe the soil depth (in feet) above a casket.

He recounted seeing beautiful bright, blinding lights, and as his sight became more focused, he was on a garden path surrounded by a foggy mist. As he walked forward, a garden gate, complete with a white trellis, came into focus. He moved faster toward that garden gate and reached to open it. He felt he needed to pass through that trellis adorned with beautiful blooming flowers.

Suddenly, his mother appeared on the other side of the garden gate and said, "Wait. Do not pass through this gate. It is not your time." He was shocked to see her and hear her message. And when his vision became even clearer, he recognized his dad, some cousins, and even an old girlfriend—all of whom had already passed. They were all there standing on the other side smiling as they reassured him, "We will all be here when you are ready."

Because of this experience, he was at peace knowing that there was something else after this life—a *reformed* atheist, so to speak. My grandfather lived another decade. He was always a nice guy during his life, and a much more peaceful man in his later years.

In what seemed like a normal evening, I enjoyed his company dining at a local Chinese restaurant—I had moo goo gai pan, as I recall. Only a few short hours later, he would suffer his final heart attack. I am certain he walked through that beautiful garden gate.

Irving: *The Gift of Time*

My former father-in-law, Irving, was the most stable person I had ever known. He toiled through jobs all his life, just to make a good living for his family. I think it came from his upbringing in a strict Jewish household, as his father was a tailor in New York City's Garment District. His mother was a Romanian immigrant. I was married to his oldest daughter (the previously mentioned Jabberwocky girl). He was an enigma to me—sometimes cranky, sometimes a jokester, sometimes angry at his bodily pain that follows most bread deliverymen into old age—but he was always generous.

Although there are many aspects to my relationship with him, I will focus on Irving's clock. It was an ordinary clock that hung high on the wall in his den, formerly the breezeway and one-car garage of a small bungalow on Long Island, NY. Remodeling the den was a labor of love for him. The large windows, skylights, knotty pine wood, high ceilings, and lots of plants made it an inviting room to spend time in and relax. The den was Irving's escape from his world of responsibilities. He could kick back, relax, work on a crossword puzzle, watch TV, have conversations, read, or just nap.

On our visits to New York, my wife (at the time) and I would always choose to sleep on the pull-out couch in that den. It was an inviting place to sleep, too. Surrounded by large plants, it felt like we were camping in a forest, as we looked through the roof's skylight windows to enjoy the few stars noticable in an overly bright Long Island night sky.

The only problem with this room was his clock. It hung high on the pine wall at the far end of the room and was the type of clock that continuously announced its presence—*tick-tock, tick-tock, tick-tock, tick-tock*—as its long brass pendulum went back and forth. During the day, we did not notice this constant keeper of time. But at night, when sleeping in the forest atmosphere, the clock would become a distraction to a peaceful night's rest. We struggled with how to solve this issue without offending Irving.

So, on one of our regular visits from Ohio, we decided to take the clock off the wall before going to bed, which prevented the pendulum from making its annoying sound. Each morning, I would reset the time, pull up a chair, hang it back on the wall, and kick-start the pendulum before Irving noticed we had fiddled with it. This procedure was successful for many trips to Long Island. But on this one fateful morning, we had forgotten to put the clock back in its proper place of honor.

Irving was quite annoyed at our procedure of disabling his clock before bedtime. He seemed hurt about our dislike for the constant *tick-tock, tick-tock, tick-tock, tick-tock* that must have brought him some comfort we could not understand. Over the years, not much else was said about our nightly deactivation of his special clock. He probably went along because his granddaughters were now part of our family visits, and they were the apples of his eye.

My father-in-law was the type of person who never went to see a doctor. He had to keep up his appearance of being the family's *Rock of Gibraltar*. On one trip to visit, he casually mentioned he had not been feeling well for quite some time. My wife, knowing her father did not mention anything like that in a casual manner, made him promise to go see a doctor. It was a shock when he was diagnosed with advanced prostate cancer, which had already spread throughout his body.

At first, he tried to keep up his strong appearance, but things changed. Upon our arrival for one of our next visits to New York, we placed our luggage in the den, which was our usual procedure. To our amazement, he had already taken the clock off the den wall! We were not sure whether to mention it or not. We went into the kitchen, and he said with a smile, "Did you notice anything in the den?" We said, "Thank you, but next time he didn't have to take the clock down by himself since we had become experts at the procedure." We laughed together. He was no longer worried about the little things that used to annoy him. He was much more relaxed about life. He was dying of cancer.

There were many other changes during his last two years as he fought valiantly through experimental cancer treatment sessions. He bought a cabin on a lake, nestled in the Catskill Mountains, which he had always wanted to do. We would meet there as often as we could. The stresses of life were absent as we spent hours sitting on the deck, fishing from his little boat, or watching the sunset over the lake as the loons called out their presence. We just enjoyed being together. No hurry. No hustle and bustle of life's daily distractions.

One of my fondest memories was the last visit to the cabin. He was so weak. He asked if I would set up the boat—which meant carrying the little motor and battery down the hill to the dock—a task he had always performed himself. I was honored that he asked. My oldest daughter, he, and I spent that sunny day fishing on Lake Jefferson. Hardly a word was said all day. I can't even remember if we caught any fish. I do remember that it was the last time we were together. It was so very peaceful.

During the trip to New York to his funeral, I thought about the last two years of his life. He was a different person. He was doing *soul work*—appreciating the important things in life, being with family, not becoming annoyed at the little things, doling out a large supply of kisses and hugs to his granddaughters, sitting in a boat fishing with no concept of time.

I appreciated the gift he had received. His terminal illness gave him the opportunity to choose. To choose to live out the rest of his life in bitterness and fear, or to live out the rest of his life with love—in love with life itself. I was thankful he had chosen love, and we were the beneficiaries of his choice.

This time, our trip to Long Island seemed long. As we entered the house that my wife had grown up in, it seemed empty without his presence. We all sat in the kitchen that evening and talked. I don't think anyone wanted to be in *his* den, the usual gathering place for conversation. We still decided to sleep there, as we had done for the last ten years.

At bedtime, I performed my usual ritual of pulling up a chair and carefully removing the clock from its place on his wall. I smiled as I remembered the last time we had visited and Irving had already taken the clock down, even in his weakened state. As usual, I gently carried the clock into the next room and laid it flat on the white living room carpet. My eyes welled up with tears as I recalled all the drama that had surrounded this stupid clock over the last decade. We got into the pull-out bed and fell asleep. Sometime in the middle of the night, we both awoke suddenly and laid there for a minute.

I had goosebumps. "Your father is here with us in the den," I said. My wife replied, "I know, I feel him too," and she started to cry softly. Suddenly, I heard the clock! *Tick-tock, tick-tock, tick-tock, tick-tock*. "Do you hear that?" I asked her. She responded with slight annoyance, "Yeah, you forgot to take the clock off the wall." I assured her that, after ten years, I would never forget to take the clock down.

Tick-tock, tick-tock, tick-tock, tick-tock, the clock continued to beckon us like an Edgar Allan Poe poem. My wife proposed, "Maybe you forgot to lay the clock flat, and it's still working in the living room." We got out of bed and ventured quietly into the living room. There the clock laid, flat on the floor, not working—as quiet as when I laid it there earlier in the evening. "It's Dad," she said matter-of-factly. I replied, "Yeah, in his own special sense-of-humor way he is telling us he is okay." We hugged each other and went back to sleep in his den.

At Irving's funeral, I spoke with love in my heart. I thanked him for accepting me like a son. I was especially happy he had these last two years, which had changed his outlook on life. A gift of indefinable magnitude that he gave to us. Most importantly, I reassured him we would be okay. I did not want him to feel like he had to stay here, on Earth, to watch over us. He spent most of his physical life taking care of his family. It was his time to move on to the hereafter. All of us will leave this physical life. Some of us will suddenly leave, some of us will leave earlier than expected, and some of us will leave at the conclusion of a terminal illness. I am making no judgments regarding the different manners in which we choose to leave this physical realm—each journey has its lessons to be learned, each one is part of our soul work.

When diagnosed with a terminal illness, each one of us has choices to make, a universe of potential reactions. It is the gift of time that gives each of us the opportunity to redefine who we are. It gives us the opportunity to re-do, un-do, do for the first time, or do nothing.

It is your own choice how to use this gift, as is true with any aspect within the gift we call life. Will you choose to live in fear or love? Will you choose to be bitter or thankful? Will you curse God or praise God? Will you act in accordance with God's grandest version of who you really are? You have the free will to choose. Like Irving, I pray that you choose love.

Clara: *A Gift from Heaven*

As I have already written about earlier in this book, Nan and Pop D, my maternal grandparents, were a stabilizing factor for my younger siblings and me. By the time Nan passed at age eighty-nine, her grandchildren were spread across America—but we all came together to honor her.

As we sat silently, deep within our own thoughts at her service, the reverend began, "We are here today to honor and remember a fine woman—salt of the earth." He recounted our family tradition of looking at the full moon, which we would call the "Nanny moon," and we would send our loving thoughts to her. It was like a long-distance hug.

As we drove to the Poughkeepsie Cemetery, where she was to be buried near Great-grandma Schrauth, gray clouds were rolling in. It had started to rain. I hoped someone had brought umbrellas. As we pulled up to the Schrauth family cemetery plot, I never really realized how pretty it was, sitting up on a hill with a big old oak tree nearby. The large granite stone with the engraved Schrauth name announced to all that this was the place Nan would rest in peace.

As six of us unloaded the casket, I remember thinking, *Nan was on the larger size, and could we get her safely to her resting place in the rain, up a wet and slippery hill?* I said a little prayer for strength and solid footing. She deserved a peaceful trip up that hill. Funny, the thoughts that go through your mind at a funeral.

Once she was safely in place, and our umbrellas in hand, the reverend started the proceedings. At about the time he was reciting Psalm 23, ". . . Yea, though I walk through the valley of the shadow of death, I will fear no evil: for thou art with me . . ." I had tuned out and fallen into a world of my own thoughts. *This rain reflects how I feel, and the tears are falling from Heaven. Like God is crying because Nan has died.*

I paused my thoughts for a moment to hear the reverend again, "... and I will dwell in the house of the Lord forever." *Oh wait, I am thinking about this all wrong. Nan was an awesome Christian woman, and Heaven isn't crying at all. We may be sad here on Earth that Nan has passed, but Heaven is rejoicing*! I was instantly filled with joy, and it burst out on my face with a big smile. Nan was in Heaven with God. Nan was in Heaven with Great-grandma Schrauth. I tilted my head down a bit so that no one else, with their very solemn faces, would see the smile and joyful look on my face.

At that very moment, I heard Nan call my name, *David! David!* Just like when we were little kids walking to Ethyl's house and I would run ahead. I tilted my head back up and glanced toward the big old oak tree. That's the direction I heard her calling my name from. I searched the wet branches and leaves, wondering what kind of joke this was, or maybe expecting to see Nan sitting on a sturdy oak branch watching the proceedings below.

I saw nothing. But again, I heard, *David! David!* Nan's voice seemed to be coming from up in the gray sky next to the old oak tree. I looked up and saw the most beautiful sight. The dark, gray clouds dumping rain on us instantly parted, and through that pouring rain came a beam of light. It shined all the way down into the cemetery creating the most beautiful, colorful rainbow I had ever seen in my life—even to this day. It was breathtaking.

I knew this was a gift from Nan, with a little help from God. She was telling me I was right that Heaven was wonderful. Nan's cup runneth over and overflowed right into that cemetery and filled my heart with joy.

Many years later, I was talking with my sister, Karen, about Nan's funeral. "I need to tell you something that happened at Nan's funeral," I stated with some trepidation. Her immediate response was, "Yes! Wasn't that weird!" I was taken aback by her reaction. "I know what I'm about to say," I replied with curiosity, "but what weird event are *you* referring to?"

"When Nan called out your name," she said, as if we had talked about this dozens of times throughout our lives. *She heard that*, I thought. "Yes, matter of fact, I was standing on one side of you and our uncle was on the other side. He looked at me right away. I could tell he heard it, too. Later that day, he and I agreed to never tell you, because we thought Nan was calling you to your death," she recounted.

I laughed and replied, "No. Just the opposite." I asked my sister if she had seen anything, and she said no. I thanked her for sharing, confirmed that I did indeed hear Nan calling my name at her funeral, and proceeded to tell my sister what a beautiful sight had occurred right after. "That must have been incredibly beautiful to see," she said. "It was a gift," I replied.

A Spiritual Perspective on Death

At the time

Each of these experiences occurred when I was in my twenty-somethings, long after my brush with death in the baseball dugout and my drowning choice to stay on Earth. So, at the time, I was not shocked, surprised, or in awe. It was peaceful knowing that these loved ones had transitioned and were reaching across the veil in their own unique ways: the awakening of an atheist; a ticking clock with a sense of humor; a rainbow on a stormy day. For you, it could be anything that connects you with a deceased loved one.

As I write today

Moments of connection with loved ones who have passed on occur as often as you'd like—or should I say as often as you think, speak, or act in a manner that activates the energy cord that binds our souls together—like plucking a guitar string. Each of us is connected through energy cords to a wide variety of other souls—our sons, daughters, grandchildren, future grandchildren, spouses, former spouses, past lives, brothers and sisters, cousins, best friends, and even that person who may have hurt you with your most painful life lesson. There is a beauty in being aware of your unbroken connection to loved ones beyond the veil.

For those who can't believe any of this is possible, that's okay. We all exist in a free-will universe where you are fully able to create any self-fulfilling prophecy that your heart desires—even the ability to be temporarily detached from the outreach and support of deceased loved ones, spirit guides, guardian angels, and God. But know this—long-held beliefs can sometimes hold us in patterns that are not supportive of our growth as spiritual beings of light.

Finding Clarity:

Am I able to accept that loved ones who have crossed over can show up in our lives in a variety of creative ways?

There are many signs loved ones can manifest from the hereafter to indicate they are in your presence—smells, appearance of animals, electricity manipulation, and so on. As your awareness grows, you will recognize them. I was once on a park bench reading *Conversations with God* by Neale Donald Walsch, and my heart filled with joy when a monarch butterfly landed right on my book and sat there for what seemed like minutes.

My dad likes to announce his presence through electricity. Most memorably, it was just hours after he passed as were making a batch of his favorite chocolate-chip cookies in his honor. Suddenly, the KitchenAid mixer turned on at high-speed causing the batch of freshly mixed chocolate chip cookie dough to fly around our kitchen. Why did I think it was him? Well, the KitchenAid was unplugged at the time! But mostly, it was a humorous reminder of an incident that had occurred years earlier:

> *After a night of partying in Ft. Lauderdale, where my dad and his third wife lived, we had all arrived home with a bad case of the munchies. That motivated us to make a batch of homemade chocolate chip cookies at two o'clock in the morning. Things went awry, and cookie dough flew all over his kitchen from the blades of a mixer. We laughed so hard. The cookies were delicious!*

My wife's mom announces her presence to us from the other side with the distinct aroma of freshly cut roses—her favorite.

My Pop D. is always nearby when I'm working on a home improvement project—especially when I'm not sure how to proceed. He was very handy in his life—a roofing contractor by trade. He whispers a potential solution into my consciousness as if I had him physically by my side with his hammer in hand.

Our perception of reality is limited by the physical tools we were born with—smell, taste, sight, sound, touch—but as sentient light beings, we have an ability to tap into our higher powers by acknowledging their existence within each of us. Become aware of the energy cords that connect us to our past, our present, and our future. Know that we are still connected—energy corded—to loved ones who have passed before us, and that connection shall lead us home, just like an eagle.

> *When an eaglet is born, it is blind because its eyeballs are like a gel, not yet fully solidified. Within a few days, the eaglet's eyes form. The amazing thing is their eyeballs form in a manner that enables them to "see" the Earth's magnetic field. It is naturally ingrained in the physical form of the eagle and enables it to find its home area from anywhere on the planet.*

It is not too difficult to believe that our own souls have that very same innate ability—to find our way home once we leave our bodies.

Please be aware that our loved ones—in transition to the next dimension—are still energy-corded to many others. It is reported that dying patients will see deceased loved ones in the room with them. Maybe even their guardian angels, or Jesus. We all may have to pass through the birth canal alone to get here, *but no one dies alone.*

As a final note, it is important to acknowledge to our loved ones, "It's okay to go now. I'll be okay. We will be together again." It is your parting gift—to free their spirit of Earthly constraints and concerns. So, speak the truth. Help them transition in peace.

Daily Affirmation

I shall live each moment fully present and be at peace upon my arrival into the next realm.

"The Ego seeks to divide and separate.

Spirit seeks to unify and heal."

~ Pema Chodron
American Tibetan Buddhist

Chapter Eleven

Lost and Found Redux

A Spiritual Perspective on Ego

Move Aside Spoiled Child

David K. Munson ©2021

The ego rules the roost like a spoiled child,
and hijacks perception
like a horse gone wild.

Yet you insist that what you see is real,
an attempt to encourage
your hurt ego to heal.

I see black, and you only see white,
because ego separates us,
and neither is right.

So let your ego move aside,
look past your fears that divide.
Open your eyes and see with your heart,
and don't let the ego split us apart.

Success has a way of distracting us. When the opportunity presented itself, I became a business owner. Over time, my company grew into a multimillion-dollar business with twenty-five employees. We traveled all over the United States cleaning up toxic waste, mostly for Fortune 100 companies. Early on, I thanked God for helping me achieve the goals I promised when I was drowning in Wappinger Creek. I was thankful Nathaniel was on this journey with me, too. I always said a prayer to protect the guys going out on company projects—especially when a jobsite mistake could cost somebody their life. And we did many of those types of cleanups. To this day, I am sincerely grateful all my employees always went home safely to their families.

As I became busy with the success, I gradually forgot that God, the Universe, and Nathaniel were still with me. Financial rewards, a big house, and a big ego followed. I had forgotten that none of this was possible without them. I had forgotten to include God in my thoughts. I forgot to converse with Nathaniel. I forgot to live a life of gratitude. I did not understand the ego can lead us into situations that are empty of God. I forgot to pray. I did not understand why I was not fulfilled. I was lost and didn't even know it.

At some point, the company's fortunes, and my life's path, started to shift. It was so gradual, and I didn't see the signs foretelling of company disaster. My ego wouldn't let me. Eventually, it got so bad

I had to admit to myself that I was no longer in control of my life, once again.

So, I re-engaged with Nathaniel. I started praying again—mostly the day before payroll—and many times, an unexpected check arrived, or a company would pay their invoices early—just in the exact amount needed to meet payroll that week for all the families that depended on the company's success.

Eventually everything came crashing down—hard. No more company. I remember the exact day I came to the realization I had failed—failed my clients, failed my employees, failed my family, and failed myself. My ego was devastated. I didn't want to go right home, so I drove to a local park, sat on the bench near Buttermilk Falls, and cried.

On my way home, I felt like my life was over. I was worth more dead than alive, as I had a multi-million-dollar accidental death life insurance policy. As I drove my black Honda sedan down the steep hill on Route 6, I saw an opportunity. At the bottom of the hill was the high bridge over the Chagrin River. I could just make it like I fell asleep and drive right off the road, free falling into a one-hundred-foot drop right into the river. If the crash didn't kill me, maybe I would just drown in the river. I had been there before and could choose differently. My family would then be financially taken care of.

In the five seconds it took to drive down that hill, thinking those thoughts about ending my life, I targeted the exact spot I would have to aim the car. I certainly didn't want to go off the road and fail at this final task. I needed to ensure that I would die. About twenty feet from that perfect launching spot, just before the bridge, Nathaniel implored to me, "No, David. Don't do that!" I broke out of my focus on suicide and straightened the car back into my driving lane. Nathaniel had never failed to give me insights for my highest good. So, I drove home.

That summer, I would go outside into the garden many times. For me, gardening was meditative, reduced my stress, and took my mind off losing my multimillion-dollar environmental cleanup company. Gardening helped me deal with the frustration that I couldn't even find an executive-level position anywhere else.

I was in the front yard of my large home with the for sale sign by the street, under the flowering plum tree I had planted a year earlier, when Nathaniel stated, in no uncertain terms, "David, it's time to write your book." Not that I wanted to seem contradictory, but I had to ask, "What book?" Nathaniel continued matter-of-factly, "The reason you came here—to this life—at this time.

To write the book." *Hmmm*, I thought. Throughout that summer, Nathaniel would remind me often that it was time. So, I relented and started writing the first chapter.

Even though I started writing, that summer was an emotional roller coaster. I was looking for an executive-level position, but they were few and far between. It seemed like I was always the second-best candidate. As I drove in and out of my neighborhood through some side streets with smaller houses (the older part of the neighborhood), I always passed this white, Cape Cod-style house where the lawn had not been mowed in quite some time. It looked shabby. And I was angry. How could I sell my house at the end of the street (where the newer, bigger houses were) if potential buyers had to drive by this unkempt home? It was a symbol of how frustrated I was with life—so I silently cursed the owner every time I passed by.

The low point was when I went to my third interview at a small, privately owned manufacturing company. I was very well qualified and felt like the leading candidate. At the second round of interviews, they put me through two hours of testing—math, management style, engineering, leadership style, accounting stuff—the whole gamut. On that day, the human resources manager told me the results of my testing—no one had ever scored as high as I did on those tests. She was very impressed. I had this job in the bag, I thought. We wouldn't have to sell the house. We were down to our last mortgage payment in the bank. The Universe was working its magic—or so I thought. Her next statement shocked me. "So, we will not be offering you the position, because the company owner said he would not hire someone smarter than him." I was shocked and angry when I left.

I was still fuming as I passed by the lazy neighbor's house with the lawn not mowed—which made me even angrier at the owner of that house. "Why can't they keep their yard looking nice, damn it," I yelled out loud.

Then I saw it—I mean her. This frail, gray-haired woman who was hunched over trying to push her lawnmower. She had progressed down the first row of grass with one arm pushing the lawnmower and the other leaning on a cane. She was struggling, as the grass had gotten to be nearly a foot high by this point in the summer. I felt so bad, so guilty for cursing her out all summer just because my own life was a freaking mess. I had to re-evaluate everything. I had to re-evaluate my perceptions of life. My anger. My judgment. My thoughts about how things had turned badly so quickly. I tossed and turned all night.

In the morning, I woke up and fired up my nearly new John Deere riding mower and proceeded down the street. When I arrived at her house, I could see that she had only completed one row of grass—out of more than an acre of lawn! So, I started down the second row of tall grass, and the John Deere was easily doing its job. By the time I was halfway done with the front yard, the frail-looking, gray-haired woman with a cane—wearing a bathrobe and slippers—was walking down her sidewalk toward me. I figured she was coming to thank me.

"Who are you!" she yelled. "Why are you mowing my lawn?" I was taken aback by her tone and replied, "I'm your neighbor from down the street. I drove by yesterday, saw you struggling, and thought I would help." With a small hint of a smile, she said "Oh. I thought maybe my son sent you for my birthday tomorrow." I replied no, as I wondered why her son wasn't there mowing the lawn for her. "Well then, thank you. I didn't know there were people like you still left in this world," she shared. "I'm glad to help," I replied. "And happy birthday!" She smiled, turned around, leaned on her cane once again, and disappeared back into her home.

As I completed mowing the front yard, I was smiling because I hadn't felt this good inside for a long time. Maybe I should change careers—go into something that helps people now that my career in cleaning up the environment appeared to be over. *That felt right*, I thought, just as the first raindrops started. But it's her birthday present, so here we go! I pressed the gas pedal and mowed that back yard in the pouring rain—with a big smile on my face. I had a new outlook on life. A new perspective. I thanked Nathaniel for opening my eyes to new possibilities.

The next morning, I opened the Sunday paper to view the employment ads and decided to read them all for new possibilities that my ego hadn't allowed in the past few months. And there it was, "*Do you want to help people in need in our community? Join United Way as a temporary campaign fundraiser.*" Thank you, Nathaniel. If my eyes hadn't been opened, I would not have seen this opportunity.

Twenty-four hours later, I was a campaign representative for United Way. In just six short months, I had gone from a company executive making the present equivalent of $250,000 per year to a temporary fundraiser at $10.00 per hour. I knew I was on the right path. I knew this was the Universe guiding me to where I was to go. Over the next eleven fundraising campaigns, I helped raise more than $30 million dollars for people in need. I had set my ego aside and listened to my heart—and Nathaniel.

A Spiritual Perspective on Ego

At the time

It wasn't long after I accepted the temporary, nonprofit job that our family funds had dwindled down to nothing. The bank was threatening to repossess one of our vehicles. I was praying a lot. I was reconnecting with Nathaniel. Just trying to keep things together. I recall clearly that there was only enough money in the bank for one more mortgage payment, and the house was still on the market. The real estate agent let us know houses in our price range could take up to six months to sell, especially in the middle of winter.

After a few weeks, we were discouraged that not one family had come to see the house. I prayed. I prayed that the family destined to enjoy this big, beautiful home would appear the following weekend. That Friday night, a snowstorm hit Northeast Ohio—really, a blizzard—because by Saturday morning there was more than a foot of snow on the ground, and it was still accumulating. In that moment, I had lost faith.

Later that afternoon, the phone rang, "Are you the owner of the home for sale at [. . .]" I responded, "Yes, why do you ask?" The caller replied, "Well, my wife and I are sitting in our car in front of your house right now. You probably can't see us because it's snowing so hard at the moment. But we are only in town for the weekend from

Pennsylvania looking at houses and had a feeling we should drive down this street," he admitted.

We invited them into the house, snow-covered boots, and all! Two days later we accepted their offer to buy our home. An answer to my sincere prayer. An end to a chapter in our lives, but a renewal of faith. As I look back, I had lost my business, found a new calling, re-established a relationship with my guardian angel, Nathaniel, and found God again—a trade I would make every time.

As I write today

Over the past few decades, I have been able to acknowledge my own talents, skills, and intellect—not to feed my ego as in the past—but to acknowledge them as blessings endowed upon me to complete my soul plan in this lifetime. To merely be a messenger.

We are on the precipice of a massive shift in humanity. Will we set aside our egos, which served us well when we were at the lower rungs of the Maslow hierarchy of needs? It is time to acknowledge and accept that the next greatest ascension in human existence is arriving. Not like the discovery of fire, which provided physical shelter and security for our ancient ancestors. Not like the Renaissance, a period that jump-started humanity into the great scientific advancement that has continued into this modern era. More akin to the spiritual awakening after Jesus was crucified and there was an awareness of the true nature of the human soul, as separate from our bodies.

At present, this spiritual awakening is an energy shift toward the recognition that we are all one—all connected. We are all part of Universal energy. The shift will occur when we remember it is—and always has been—available and accessible to each of us.

It is a spiritual awakening into our *Individual Access to the Matrix of Quantum Universal Energy (IAMQUE)*. But if it makes you more comfortable, we can refer to it as the awakening into The Golden Age of only-love.

This transition to IAMQUE has already begun on our planet. A shift to greater conscious awareness of our true energetic nature, as beings of light. Initially, this shift is going to be very chaotic for a variety of reasons. Many of us will not understand how to intellectually process, interpret, or emotionally incorporate the awakening of energetic awareness, within ourselves. Unfortunately, our natural abilities have been suppressed for most of human history.

Some people will be totally unaware. Some people will act in ways, both positive and negative, that we have never experienced before. Some people will revel in the shift, because deep down they have been waiting for it. Some of us already chose to come to Earth at this time just to assist in this awakening.

Finding Clarity:
Am I able to remember why I am here?

As with any shift in human history, there will be those people who will fight to remain in control, remain in a system that feeds their own egos with power and money. The elite class will hoard resources that are perceived to be limited, at the expense of the rest of us. I think Machiavelli explained it best in his book, *The Prince*, written in 1513:

> *"It ought to be remembered that there is nothing more difficult to take in hand, more perilous to conduct, or more uncertain in its success, than to take the lead in the introduction of a new order of things. Because the innovator has for enemies all those who have done well under the old conditions, and lukewarm defenders in those who may do well under the new. This coolness arises partly from fear of the opponents, who have the laws on their side, and partly from the incredulity of men, who do not readily believe in new things until they have had a long experience of them."*

Machiavelli pointed out a truth about how the ego protects the status quo. But what will the chaos look like in the twenty-first century, as those in power protect their ego-driven agendas? They will create, or add to, the confusion, sickness, separation, and fear felt by souls not already in vibrational alignment with the arriving spiritual shift.

So, here we are today in 2023. I know many spiritual people who believe that by ignoring or not acknowledging the existence of evil, it will just disappear. They have said to me, "Don't give it the energy of your thoughts." From my perspective, that viewpoint appears to be silent consent, but maybe they are more enlightened than me. I'm just not sure how to pray to fix something that is un-acknowledged.

I agree that it is much more peaceful to ignore the chaos. Sometimes—*just for brief moments*—I wish I had the ability to click into naivety and bliss. But that's not my individual path. Because I acknowledge that to not take action to defeat the darkness taking control in our world might be construed by a literal Universe as passive acceptance. And that is exactly how light is extinguished.

I believe that the collective consciousness of humanity's intent toward a common beneficial outcome is the most powerful force in the Universe.

So, from my perspective, I find it uncomfortable that I must point out exactly what the messy and chaotic—the darkness draining our souls—looks like in today's world. I didn't want to do that in this book, but Spirit has urged me to be one of the many messengers. To awaken humanity. To present a choice. To be collectively conscious.

So here goes. . .

We are in a spiritual war. A battle for the collective souls of humanity. And yes, God is our leader, but we chose to come to a dimension that accepts individual free will over an Almighty who *dictates* change. So, know this—our world will only change course away from the darkness when the collective consciousness of all light beings actively co-manifest a new path—*together*. In a weird sort of way, it's *spiritual groupthink*—using the term in a beneficial manner.

Separatism and the Ego

Just think how the world would be if we set aside our egos and our perceived differences. It may seem like an impossible task to motivate people to do this, to dissolve the false walls of separation. To become connected souls living in a physical time-space dimension that exemplifies only-love. An existence where souls in the herebefore would be proud to experience. Together, we can overcome not-love, but only if we recognize its existence and call out all the weapons of Separatism.

For me, I cannot stand idly by. As we separate from each other, we must ask ourselves: Am I separating myself from other beings of light because I desire that; Or have I allowed others to coerce me into the darkness of the *Separatism Movement*.

It's time to awaken to the subtle, and sometimes not-so-subtle, methods implemented to separate us—physically, emotionally, politically, and spiritually—as a strategic method to divide, conquer, and control. You may recognize, or be an unsuspecting casualty of, how the Separatism Movement has crept into our society:

[*Insert latest pandemic*] as **separation** from each other by six feet

[*Insert any color*] Lives Matter, as **separation** by race

[*Insert hidden school agenda*], as **separation** of children and parents

[*new acronym m.a.p. for pedophiliacs*], as **separation** from morality

[*Insert biological male in women's sport*], as **separation** from fairness

[*Insert name of porn website*], as **separation** from healthy relationship

[*Insert name of latest banned book*], as **separation** from knowledge

[*Insert college banned guest speakers*], as **separation** from free speech

[*Insert newest tech device*], as **separation** from personal privacy

[*Insert latest weather event*], as **separation** from scientific discourse

[*Insert statue that has been torn down*], as **separation** from history

[*Insert legal weapon ban*], as **separation** of protection against tyranny

The Separatism Movement has fractured us into a million disjointed groups. We have been fed a steady diet of fear. And fear is the most effective tool of separatism. When people are confused, sick, and especially separated, fear is very simple to insert into our society by those who desire control, power, and money. We have been tricked, and our egos willingly participate, or at a minimum, we have been led away from the truth of our Oneness.

Can we continue to live as proverbial jellyfish tossed about by the storms, while others relax on their yachts above the fray? It is all a manipulation, and many of us are the lab rats running on a spinning wheel that goes nowhere. A spinning wheel that distracts each of us from just saying, "Stop the madness! Stop suppressing the truth! Stop telling us we are separate! Stop telling us we are not enough!" Because the truth of the Universe is that we lack nothing. But at this moment in human history, we do lack awareness. And we lack the unity to shine our light on the Separatism Movement in America.

The mass of humanity needs to reconnect on a spiritual level, or we are all destined to be slaves to our separation—and slaves to the darkness. It is time to see each other as beings of light. It is time to nurture and empower each other to bring light energy into our bodies. To raise our vibrational frequency. To stand together, united as unique individuals, all connected with one purpose—to end the charade of separation—to stop the Separatism Movement's agenda.

The American Dream and the Ego

I used to believe in the American dream—good education, steady job, a house, and family. And my ego was a willing partner in the quest to attain all those things—sometimes the bigger the better. Now, I redefine the American Dream as freedom from life-long financial servitude. Freedom to choose what is best for my family.

Observing senior citizens working at McDonalds and Walmart for minimum wage to make ends meet has opened my eyes. In America, the financial systems are constructed to maintain control of the population—at all ages and at all levels of income—except the elite.

In a familiar scenario, children are encouraged to go to college, start a career, have a family, and purchase a home—historical foundations of the perceived American Dream. According to *educationdata.org*, the annual cost of college tuition and fees in public institutions increased 382% from 1980 to 2020—and that's inflation adjusted! The financial burden of a college education has nearly quadrupled over that period. Young people just getting started in life are already indebted to the government/banking partnership system.

And then they jump from the frying pan into the fire by purchasing a new car and signing up for a loan—on an item that loses 10% of its value as you drive it off the lot. Falling deeper into the financial trap.

Here's the worst part. The largest scam ever perpetrated on the American people is home mortgages. The sales pitch is *"only 5% to 6% annual interest over a thirty-year period. If you invest in the stock market, your financial returns will more than make up for the interest rate."* Until the reality sets in after you buy your first house at $250K with a 5% interest rate from the very friendly and helpful banker—whose risk is minimized by government guarantees. And you happily give away 6% of your home's value to a realtor who maybe spent a few days helping you find that dream home. That's a financial scam that should go away, too.

After the first month in your newly purchased home, you will see this—only 23% of your payment went toward loan payoff with the other 77% of your hard-earned money going to the financial institution as an interest payment. And you thought the mortgage loan was only 5% annual interest rate. Over the 30-year life of that loan, you will have paid $233K in interest payments on a $250K loan—*a 48% interest rate*. Welcome to the financial slavery system of home mortgages.

As you read this today, large companies in our country are buying up homes with cash—consolidating the real estate market under one elite umbrella. Their goal—allow *no one* to own their own homes—they collect rent forever! Just the next step in financial slavery. And the fair solution would be so easy—require the financial banking system to charge just a straight fee—not compounded interest. They will yell *risk, risk, risk*, but they still hold onto your deed as collateral. End financial slavery. End the elite corporate take-over of the housing market.

And when politicians promised to relieve your student loans—*really by transferring your debt onto other taxpayers*—it's not out of the goodness of their hearts. They are not only buying your vote, but freeing your finances up so you can jump into their mortgage trap. As the fish learned in an earlier metaphor—there is no such thing as a free lunch. There are always unforeseen consequences.

On the other side of the same financial coin are those who cannot afford the above-described way of life in America. Ultimately, they fall into the financial trap of increasing government financial dependence to survive their daily existence. Financial slavery in

America is a two-headed dragon. And "*we the people*" unwittingly feed that dragon. We cannot be spiritually free while caught in this invisible trap. We can only *perceive* freedom.

Unshackling from the daily burdens of financial stress opens the door for the building of our personal and collective spiritual wealth. So, let's welcome the Quantum Financial System as soon as possible. It will end our financial slavery. If you are interested in real financial freedom, do your own research. I recommend starting with David Ramsey's best-seller, *The Total Money Makeover – A Proven Plan for Financial Fitness*.

Representative Government and the Ego

Our perception is that Congress represents the people, but is that true? There are some politicians who talk a good game, especially around election time. And many new to the political game do have good intentions of helping the little guy . . . the average Joe on the street. But let's be real—it takes millions and millions of dollars to get elected in the United States. By the time these idealistic representatives get to Congress, they have spent so much money and made so many promises that they unwittingly become indebted to a rigged political system. And political and financial pressures mount, crushing their egos. Crushing their good intentions to represent us.

According to the website *OpenSecrets.org*, more than half of Congress (Senate and House of Representatives) are millionaires based upon 2018 data. On the other side of this coin, less than 10% of Americans fall into this category. Are they really representative of their constituencies? And the trend is that the longer you serve in Congress the richer you get. How does that happen? Lobbyists.

OpenSecrets.org data also shows that 12,000 lobbyists spent more than $4 billion dollars—just in 2022—convincing politicians to "see it their way." Each lobbyist is spending on average $333,333 *every year* to influence our representatives. Money flows. Loyalty to special interests grows. Who is in Washington, D.C. protecting the average citizen? The tail is wagging the dog. And our own egos continue to believe that we live in a free country. How do we fix this?

By enacting term limits, reforming campaign finance laws, and outlawing lobbyists would be a great new start to regain our representative government "*of the people, by the people, and for the people*" to quote President Lincoln's Gettysburg Address. It's as true today as it was in 1863. There is an enormous amount of information about our politicians on *opensecrets.org*. Check it out for yourselves.

Cultural Defeat and the Ego

Let me go back to another time in our history when a major shift occurred—when groups of people defined themselves as separate, and their egos would not let them join together. Based upon this concept, I could describe much of human history where civilizations were altered by an unforeseen *cultural shift*. A more recent historical example is the decimation of the Native American population:

In the 16th century, there was an estimated two million Native Americans living in what is now the United States—some sources estimate even more throughout North America. We discuss them as Native Americans, but in those days, they lived in more than five hundred separate tribes. Even in the New England area, the tribes represented a population of more than sixty thousand people—more than enough to repel the upcoming change in the course of history. Every tribe had a leader, elder, shaman, or chief who protected the legacy of their own tribe, protected their own resources, and ensured their own way of life—or so they thought. I am compelled to attach a small list of just a few of the *five-hundred tribal nations*, many that you will recognize:

Algonquin	Apache	Arapaho	Assiniboine
Blackfeet	Caddo	Calusa	Cherokee
Cheyenne	Chickasaw	Chinook	Choctaw
Chumash	Comanche	Cree	Creek
Crow	Dakota	Delaware	Erie
Flathead	Hidatsa	Hopi	Huron
Iowa	Iroquois	Kiowa	Klamath
Mandan	Menominee	Miami	Narragansett
Naskapi	Navajo	Nez Perce	Ojibwa
Oneidas	Osage	Ottawa	Pawnee
Penobscot	Pima	Pomo	Potewatamus
Powhatan	Pueblo	Querechos	Sauk
Seminoles	Shashone	Shawnee	Sioux
Tuscarora	Ute	Wampanoag	Winnebago

Looking back, it appears to me their leaders did not set aside their egos long enough to see the cultural war beginning that would ultimately destroy their way of life. Ego caused their destruction.

I am certain that many scholars will view this analysis as an oversimplification while they pontificate their theories about why the Native American culture was conquered. It only comes down to one thing—the lack of a visionary leader who could challenge and dismantle their strongly held belief in tribal separation. Someone to simply communicate that they were really One. To awaken their souls to the truth that they were stronger together but would fall one-by-one separately. Which is exactly what happened.

In a final act of control by the incoming cultural conquerors, thousands of Cherokee men, women, and children were forcibly marched from their homelands westward eight-hundred miles into Oklahoma territory in the deadly summer heat and winter snows. This was their Trail of Tears. Read more about this at *cherokeehistorical.org/trail-of-tears.*

Like the Native American tribes that fought with each other over land and resources, much to their demise in the cultural war, today's religious organizations are not united in the present-day *spiritual war*. They separate from each other even though they have a common enemy—the Godlessness in our world.

Our religious institutions, and our souls, have been under attack for a long time. I'm sure there are individual religious organizations that are fighting darkness, just like individual tribes fought the European onslaught. It is way too late for that. This war has been going on for decades: destroy the traditional Judeo-Christian family structure; take God out of the schools; ensure that political discussion cannot occur on the pulpit; create discourse between separated groups; maintain children's education under government control; bring sexual instruction out of the privacy of one's bedroom; dress as Satan and sing a popular song on television for all the world to see; and on and on and on. Who will step up on behalf of God's children? Set aside your egos and shine a collective light into the darkness.

Interestingly, some say that discussing politics from the pulpit is not allowed in the Constitution. They are incorrect. Really, Democrat Senator Lyndon Johnson, before he became vice president, was losing ground in his reelection campaign in Texas due to an upswell in religious leaders backing the opposing Republican candidate. So, in 1954 he slipped an amendment into a larger congressional bill—as part of the IRS Code, 501(c)(3)—making it illegal to discuss politics from the pulpit. He suppressed free speech to a large portion of Americans to this day. He easily won reelection. In 1960, he became vice president and is a central figure in one of the many theories about who may have planned the assassination of President John F. Kennedy—which gave Johnson the White House.

Leaders of the world religions must set aside their egos and come together as one. They must unite in their message of Oneness—because we *are* all One. Free speech must be returned to those people who love God. That light of togetherness and solidarity will overcome the darkness. On our present path, the darkness will win—*and God will be replaced by Government.* And that's their end game.

The solution is easy—repeal the Johnson Amendment and restore free speech to those of us who worship God. And let's hold a Woodstock-like revival to deposit only-love into humanity's spiritual wealth account. It's time to start today. I'll be there!

Daily Affirmation

I set aside my ego and sincerely pray to shine my light every day to dispel darkness.

"Soul groups tend to return to Earth together. We come back in different relationship combinations. They're souls we've known before and loved in past lifetimes. So, soulmates can be our best friends, parents, a beloved teacher or even our children. And of course, soulmates can also be the great loves of our lives."

~**Karen M. Black, Canadian Spiritual Author**
(republished from KarenMBlack.com)

Chapter Twelve

The Orb of White Light

A Spiritual Perspective on Soul Groups

When Souls Kiss

David K. Munson ©2010

Images of the world dissolve,
in truth, collapse the wall.
Lips onto lips,
free-falling into your eyes,
revealing only we.

As if time has stood still,
or really, never existed at all.
Energy mingled, entwined,
would I ever again find me?

What matter is it that I would be
so changed by your caress,
ourselves, soul into soul.

What wonderful creation
occurs in that moment,
and God smiles within.
How blessed are we
when our souls kiss.

In each of our individual lives, events occur that alter the life path we are on, or at the very least, offer us an option to change course. You saw these types of events in my life through-out this book, but none were as perplexing to me as the *orb of white light*.

It was the last week in July 2009—that time of year when the temporary campaign employees are trained to work on the multimillion-dollar fundraising campaign for United Way. As vice president, I oversaw that effort, and this was the start of my ninth fundraising campaign. The training sessions were typically held in an area of the building we fondly referred to as the pit. Not sure where the name came from, but it was already there when I had arrived as a temporary campaign rep eight years earlier. It was an area with multiple computer stations, a large conference table for meetings, an area used to compile campaign literature, mailings, and telephones for solicitation calls—the standard stuff of fundraising campaigns.

On this day, I was training Dianne, one of the newly hired campaign reps in the pit—each of us at one of the computer stations. As we went through procedures, spreadsheets, and predictive campaign analysis protocols, she turned around in her chair to ask me a question. I turned to the side in my chair to face her and began to listen to her question—and that's when I saw *it*.

A dime-sized orb of white light floating in the air about a foot above and behind her head. At first, I thought I was just seeing things and continued to attempt to pay attention to her question about campaign history charts. But there it remained, this orb of light floating above her head, which now had my full attention. I looked around the room thinking it was reflected sunlight, but there were no windows in the pit. I leaned forward in my chair thinking I could get a closer look and realized there was, in fact, a floating orb of white light. At the very moment I acknowledged its presence, it exploded into a rainbow of visible frequencies of light!

Suddenly, this pattern of rainbow colors—within milliseconds—was heading straight for her. I looked at her face, but she just kept talking, unaware of what was occurring. As the rainbow of colors was expanding and passing by her, her blonde hair blew forward. Her lips were moving as she continued asking her question, but I heard no sound. In the next millisecond, the colors disappeared as this light energy wave traveled the six feet between our computer stations. It looked like a blurry wave of energy—like on a very sunny summer day when the heat rises off a hot road and blurs the reality above that road. That's what this energy wave looked like, and it was heading straight for me in what seemed like slow motion.

This light energy wave hit me in my heart chakra and knocked me back in my chair. Within seconds, I realized I was not imagining this. And the energy wave contained information—deep feelings of some sort—about her life. It was as if the light wave was encoded with filaments of information.

I looked at her and her lips were still moving, but I still could hear no sound. It was like I was in an alternate reality. I didn't think *what the heck was that.* I didn't try to deny that it had happened. I just looked at her and thought, *who is she to me?* I didn't even acknowledge her question. I just stood up and went back to my office without saying a word.

Who is she to me? What was that orb of white light? Why did it travel right into my heart chakra? Why did that energy wave contain all these insights? Was that even possible? I knew that every time the Universe did something like this, my life would change in some way. With that thought, my knees began to shake as I sat in my office. I rationalized that the Universe must be telling me to be alert for a message that I was to deliver to Dianne—maybe something she needed to hear to help in her own life's journey.

As the weeks progressed during the campaign, all the temporary personnel were working hard together. Occasionally, Dianne and I would get in a conversation about some nonwork topic—cars, baseball, photography, spirituality, religion—and I would open my mind to be ready for the insight I was required to deliver. Finally, one day we got on the topic of death, and the insight became clear. She admitted she was afraid of dying alone. I already knew. That information was in the orb of white light.

I reminded her we may be born alone as our souls condense into a very small package to enter this world, but no one ever dies alone.

Past loved ones, guardian angels, etc. are all there to reach out a hand from the other side, as our loved ones on this side say good-bye, so we may release into the next dimension of life. Dianne seemed reassured by this message, and I figured I had fulfilled my duty to the Universe—and to her.

As the days stretched on through the fall 2009 United Way fundraising campaign, most days were normal. Well, as normal as fundraising gets—pledge incentives, pledge participation rates, average gifts, special events, food drives, workplace presentations, envelope stuffing, solicitations, company-by-company results, and campaign cabinet meetings.

Interspersed with the workday normalcy were moments that defied explanation, as if the orb of white light itself weren't enough to comprehend. Moments that made me wonder if I had really completed the mission the Universe had assigned to me. To solve the mystery, I would have to rely on a lifetime of angelic interactions, experiences, messages, and lessons from the unseen Universe into my lifetime reality.

Months after the orb occurred, I was in Dianne's office going over campaign materials. When we were done, she pulled out some photographs of when she went to a national street rod car convention in Louisville, KY, many years before with her current fiancé. She was showing me some of the cars. I acted interested, although cars were never my thing. When she got to the photograph of her standing next to a '48 Chevy Sedan Delivery, my attention went to the picture of her younger self. I knew her! I knew her when she was younger!

Suddenly, the table was breaking into molecules that rushed past my face. It felt like I was falling into eternity. The best I can describe it … like in *Star Trek* when Captain John Luc Picard says, "Engage," and all you see are stars whizzing past at warp speed. Like that. I put both hands right onto the table to steady myself back into reality. I just looked at her, got up, said, "I can't do this anymore," and went back to my office. I had no idea of what had just happened, but I knew we had not known each other before in *this* lifetime. Dianne recounted later that she thought she was in trouble for bringing personal pictures into the office because I left so abruptly.

Another time, we were working together planting flowers in the front garden of United Way. It was a nice sunny day and a needed distraction from the rigors of fundraising. We had already dis-cussed that we both really enjoyed gardening, especially, designing garden landscapes. Conversations continued about the gardens we had each separately worked on throughout our lives. Suddenly (*and yes, I use that word often in this chapter*), my vision shifted to another place and time. It's like my eyesight had been hijacked by a virtual reality headset. This is what I was shown.

I was in a field working the dry, hard clay in what appeared to be the Dust Bowl of the mid-1930s. In the distance, I could see a small, one-room farmhouse made of weathered, natural logs. I looked over to my left and saw Dianne with a hoe in her hand struggling in the hot, midday sun, attempting to turn that awful soil. She took off her wide-brimmed straw hat. Her short, dirty-blonde hair blew in the dusty breeze. She wiped her brow and continued to work the land. My thought was, "*Wow, she is so beautiful. This is such a hard life.*" And then my reality was back in the United Way front garden. *Why did I just have a vision of Dianne and me in another place and time*, I wondered. Dianne had no idea this just went through my head. I kept this experience to myself.

To be accurate, that wasn't the first time I had visions of other lifetimes, although Dianne wasn't in those visions. My first vision was at the Observatory, El Caracol, at Chichen Itza in the Yucatan Peninsula of Mexico, one of the sites of the vast Mayan empire. This site was always intriguing to me. I felt drawn to it, so much so that my first wife and I traveled to the Mayan Riviera for a vacation. The swimming was great. The food was excellent. But my desire was to climb the pyramid at the Chichen Itza site, which I accomplished.

As I entered the decaying, rounded dome of the Chichen Itza Observatory by myself, all I could see was the dense jungle above that had engulfed what once was a window into the ancient skies above the Mayan Empire. Then it happened. The stone-carved dome appeared intact, and I saw stars through the windows looking into the heavens. I felt very lonely, but I felt a sense of duty to understand the heavens and the movements of heavenly bodies. That was my calling in that lifetime—to protect the Mayan empire as an astronomer. Then the vision was gone, and the heat and humidity of the Mexican afternoon became quite apparent.

I left the Observatory and caught up to my wife and the tour group as they were entering the Great Ball Court. As I listened to our tour guide speculate on the type of game the Mayans may have played on this massive stone-lined field, all I could think about was that he was wrong! And the vision started again.

Suddenly, I was sitting at the far end of the Great Ball Court with the royalty, although I was there in my capacity as Observer of the Heavens. I could feel it was important, and I sensed I didn't get out much during the day. I could see the teams and their equipment. The intensity of the game was palpable as one team scored. Then my vision ended, and I was standing alone about fifty yards behind the tour group. I ran to catch up. I no longer wondered why I was drawn to this place, because I knew I had lived a lifetime here.

Years later, I was laying on a massage table. My medical massotherapist's name was David, too. He was working to relax my tense muscles and balance my chaotic energies. Suddenly, I was transported into the next vision of another lifetime. My eyes were already closed when I smelled the smoke. I opened my eyes only to see the blue sky and clouds peeking through the top of a large teepee. David was there and chanting in a language I didn't recognize but felt the healing intent. He was waving around and blowing on the white sage, the source of the healing smoke. He was my Native American brother, and we were the sons of the chief. He was the healing shaman of the tribe, and I was the warrior—the protector. I felt the same energies we brought into this lifetime, and the same brotherly love. Some things are soul deep. Later, he recounted to me that he has had similar visions. He confirmed his own belief that we are truly brotherly souls who have traveled lifetimes together.

The more I explore the depth of my own soul, it has become clear to me I have traveled lifetimes with some of the same souls—each helping the other to experience the circumstances that bring our souls to a higher level of learning—a higher vibrational level closer to the Oneness. There are many master teachers on our planet with great skills in discerning these issues, and many excellent books on how souls travel together in groups. I will leave it to you to decide how far you would like to journey down that path of knowledge—in this life, anyway.

Back to the orb of light, Dianne, and *those* visions. There were many more, but I will describe this last one during our time working together at United Way.

I had arrived in the back parking lot to start a new day, got out of my car, and started walking toward the back door when Dianne pulled in with her vehicle, a shiny, silver metallic 2002 Mitsubishi Eclipse. I decided to hold the back door open since she was already walking toward me from her car about fifty feet away. Our eyes met and we smiled. Suddenly (*there is that word, again*), all I could see was Dianne walking toward me in a wedding dress, with a beaming smile, and holding a bouquet of flowers. *What?* I could still see her car, the parking lot, and knew I was still holding the door open—all a reasonable part of my present reality. When she was about ten feet from me the vision ended, and she was walking toward me in her regular work attire. She confessed to me, many months later, that as she pulled into the parking lot that day, a voice from the Universe said to her, "Your husband is here." Although it freaked us both out, we remained silent about the events of that morning.

It had become clear to me the orb of light was not about Dianne needing to hear some pearl of wisdom from the Universe through me—but that there was a major life-change option that was presenting itself. A significant intersection, and a branching in both of our trees of life, if we each so chose individually to make that shift in our free-will lives.

Eventually, the Universe led me to understand about the seven chakras associated with the energetic field that surrounds our bodies. I learned our soul's energy is so large that it just overflows outside the denseness of our physical bodies—it is our energetic body—also called our aura. Well, it turns out there is an eighth chakra, referred to as the *soul star chakra*, which resides about one foot above our heads. It is associated with the color white—a compilation of all the rainbow of colors. It connects us to, helps us restore, rejuvenate, and balance connections to other dimensions or worlds, past lives, and spiritual healing. It is now clear the orb of white light above her head in the pit was a manifestation of energy emanating from Dianne's *soul star chakra*.

#

It was Cinco de Mayo—the fifth of May—nearly two years later. I was driving north on I-17 in Arizona with my sisters Karen and Sue, and a few friends, on our way to Sedona. We had an important event scheduled that couldn't be missed, and we were worried about parking. Finding a parking spot in downtown Sedona on a Saturday can be quite challenging—and it was also a party holiday! My sister, Sue, and I discussed options, but my go-to has always been to send a prayer into the Universe. I knew Nathaniel also tapped into that same universal energy stream and would help us out. As we approached downtown Sedona, there was a huge traffic jam. I stayed in faith. That's the key to everything—continue to have faith—sending out positive energy that the outcome of any situation, no matter how large or small, will turn out for your highest good.

Lo and behold, right in front of the Pink Jeep tours office, a car pulled out of a parking spot just as we arrived. I pulled in and thanked the Holy Spirit and Nathaniel for their help on this very special day. We all hopped into the Pink Jeeps and headed up into the red rock mountains of Sedona toward our destination.

A short time later, I stood by myself on the edge of the mesa looking into the distance trying to catch a glimpse of the last Pink Jeep driving up the bumpy, dusty road. That jeep was bringing Dianne and Reverend Sharon to our wedding ceremony. The dry, Arizona wind was blowing my suit jacket. I reached over to steady myself on the twisted juniper tree branch that also stood firmly at the edge of this cliff. I could hardly believe how beautiful the vast red rock scenery of Sedona was on this sunny day in early May. I looked back to see our friends and family gathered under the shade of a larger juniper tree awaiting the ceremony. I smiled at my sisters, who were to stand by me during the ceremony—my best women! My soul brother from many shared lifetimes, David, was there, too.

I could hardly believe that, in a few short minutes, I would be marrying my soulmate—the start of our spiritual journey together in our present life. And the culmination of many other realities together. At that moment, I felt Nathaniel nearby. He had aways been nearby. He had always helped me navigate my ups and downs as I wandered randomly through this life. And I realized in that moment, that I had not been wandering at all.

"We are all just walking each other home."

~Baba Ram Dass, American Spiritual Teacher

Epilogue

A Prayer for Humanity

One Ocean

David K. Munson ©2010

Am I not the ocean?
Am I not a stream,
Living a life of emotion,
Inner edge of the dream?

If I am but a puddle,
Or a drop of morning dew
On a blade of grass, so subtle,
as to not know I am really You.

To be, once again, of the vapours and mist,
And create a rainbow without resist.
Then rise to the heavens at the end of my night,
Aware that we are all one in God's light.

We are in a spiritual battle—maybe even the final battle for humanity. God's spiritual army—the Universe of spirit guides, guardian angels, archangels, Jesus, and the Ascended Masters—will lead the energetic shift into The Golden Age of only-love. But it can only arrive when enough people set aside their egos and add their *intent* to change what is vastly a not-love world into a more balanced existence.

What is your intent—thought, vocalized, and acted upon? Passive resistance can be easy—just withhold your support of people, companies, politicians, events, media, or nonprofits that do not align with your vision of an only-love world. Active resistance may include whatever you are spiritually motivated to implement—activism, prayer, support of your time, talent, and dollars to those who are the brave spiritual warriors during these times.

When we pray together, co-create together, and reenergize together, we break the bonds of separation as we tap into our *Individual Access to the Matrix of Quantum Universal Energy.* Your mind will thank you for it. Your body will thank you for it. Your soul will thank you for it. All of us who desire the shift into The Golden Age of only-love will thank you for it.

You can still find peace within the chaos. You can still rest within the eye of the hurricane. Here's how. The Universe gave me this prayer for you to read aloud, with sincere intent, each day:

Dear Lord,

Thank you for all your blessings in my life.

Thank you for bestowing your blessings upon others.

Thank you for allowing me the courage to change my perspective.

Thank you for granting courage to those souls who protect our innocent.

Thank you for opening the eyes of those souls who would remain blinded.

Thank you for opening the hearts of those souls who would remain aloof.

Thank you for guiding us to shine our light to dispel darkness.

Thank you for teaching humanity how to love each other.

Thank you for leading us into The Golden Age.

Amen.

When many souls pray together, separation ends. When separation ends, we are a force together. This is *their* greatest fear. When everyone shines the light of truth on our present reality, the darkness of control disperses. This is a plea to save humanity. A collective consciousness will change our perspective, bring our perception into true focus, and then we can change the world together.